101 REASONS WHY YOU ARE AWESOME

Embrace Your Uniqueness, Celebrate Your Strengths, and Discover the Reasons Why You Are Truly Amazing!

JAMIE MYERS

ISBN: 978-1-957590-46-2

For questions, email: Support@AwesomeReads.org

Please consider writing a review!

Just visit: AwesomeReads.org/review

FREE BONUS

SCAN TO GET OUR NEXT BOOK FOR FREE!

Table of Contents

INTRODUCTION

101 Reasons Why You Are Awesome was designed for those on an amazing journey of self-discovery and growth. Within this book, you'll acknowledge and explore the fantastic qualities that make you who you are.

Life is an adventure, and everybody brings something special to the table.

In this book, you'll find encouragement, affirmations, and inspiration to embrace your individuality, strengths, and quirks. Each reason is a gentle reminder that you are exceptional just the way you are, and your presence in this world is valuable beyond measure.

There may be attributes listed that you don't possess *yet.* Don't let these discourage you! They're a great source of inspiration. Just pick the ones you like the best and try to implement them into your daily life!

[1]
THERE'S NO ONE ELSE LIKE YOU

It's hard to imagine that with the billions of people in the world, there is no one else quite like you — but it's true. Many others might look similar, share your interests, and even prefer the same flavor of ice cream. However, no matter how alike people are, no two individuals are the same. This is part of the beauty of living in this world and knowing that just being who you are makes you unique and very special.

Even identical twins, who are as biologically alike as possible, are still unique individuals. They have different fingerprints, personality traits, goals, and dreams, even if they look exactly alike. Our genes and biological characteristics determine a lot about us, such as our eye color, how tall we are, and our blood type. However, our thoughts, experiences, and feelings make us complex individuals that nobody can replicate. This is one of the wonderful aspects of being human because it means we can expand our minds, develop strengths, and make an impact in the world that is singular and unrepeatable.

It can be difficult sometimes when we feel like we are different from others in how we look, speak, or think. Most people prefer to "fit in" and feel accepted rather than stand out, which is understandable. However, with time and experience, we often realize that our differences are what makes us special and appreciated by others. The world would be quite boring if everyone were the same. So, it's important to remember that the number one reason you are awesome is simply that you are who you are, and there is nobody else who is exactly like you.

[2]
YOUR SMILE
HAS POWER

Your smile is one of the most special things about you, and when you smile at others, it can brighten their day. Research has found that smiling is contagious. This means when someone notices your smile, their brain interprets your facial expression and will often mimic it—the same way you might yawn if you see someone else yawning.

Humans are biologically programmed to smile as a basic facial expression; babies usually start smiling at around six to twelve weeks old. However, some people don't smile quite as often or as openly at others as they get older. This could be due to their emotions or other feelings, culture, the way they were raised, and even genetic factors. Even if you don't receive a smile in return, it's very likely that the person still appreciates the smile you gave them.

There might be moments or days that you don't feel much like smiling, and that's understandable. However, if you decide that you want to get your smile back quickly, you can do things to help. For example, you can think of a good memory, like a vacation or holiday, or imagine something happy, like a rainbow or puppies playing. Spending time with people you know can bring your smile back as well, especially loved ones, such as friends or family.

You might even find someone you don't know smiling at you, and that could make you smile back without realizing it.

The act of smiling has been shown to improve our moods, help us feel positive, and even reduce stress or pain. Imagine the power you have to brighten someone's day with your awesome smile!

[3]
THE OBSTACLES YOU'VE OVERCOME MAKE YOU STRONGER

No one wishes for adversity or obstacles, but problems—both small and large—will inevitably come our way. Part of being prepared for these situations is to expect challenges and believe that you have the resources, strength, and perseverance to overcome them. This is especially true if you are pursuing an important long-term goal.

When you are in the middle of facing challenges, it might seem difficult to overcome them, and even more unlikely that you'll grow stronger because of them. These feelings are reasonable and to be expected in such moments. However, it's also important to remember that you have overcome trials before and that your resilience and resourcefulness will continue to carry you through.

Another thing to keep in mind, no matter how many obstacles you've faced or how strong you feel, is that you aren't alone. Sometimes, when we experience difficult circumstances, we can feel isolated or reluctant to ask for help. However, part of cultivating personal strength is utilizing all available resources and consulting others. Think of all the people you know who might have faced similar obstacles and how happy they would be to give you advice or lend a hand. There are many people we can turn to for support when we need it, including family, friends, teachers, counselors, and professionals. Sometimes, just discussing or explaining a problem can give you ideas or clear directions for overcoming it.

The obstacles you overcome and the strength you gain as you pursue your goals will help you develop important skills and knowledge for the future. The path won't necessarily be easy, but with each challenge, you will learn about yourself and take pride in your ability to persevere.

[4]
YOU'RE COMPASSIONATE

Compassion and empathy are two of the most important characteristics a person can have. When you are compassionate and empathetic to those around you, it shows that you care about others and value their feelings.

Being compassionate means feeling and showing concern for others. Humans are generally compassionate toward people who have suffered a natural disaster such as a fire, earthquake, or flood, and they will often come together to raise money and organize other ways to help. People can feel compassion for animals or the earth, and this might lead them to adopt a stray pet or volunteer to do a community clean-up.

You don't have to take part in a grand gesture to show how compassionate you are. You demonstrate compassion every day through little things such as listening, smiling, and helping others when you can. These small gestures can add up to make everything better around you.

Empathetic people demonstrate that they can understand and share how another person feels. In a way, empathy is an even deeper level of compassion. When you are empathetic, it shows that you are not only concerned for the feelings of another but that you have learned to understand how they feel. For example, you might see someone who is frustrated because they are having a difficult day. Showing empathy toward that person might mean offering to help, being extra patient with them, or doing something kind because you recognize and understand their feelings.

Many people describe the capacity for empathy as being able to "put yourself in someone else's shoes." This is a way of explaining that when you are empathetic, you are willing to see the world from another's viewpoint and develop a greater understanding of them and their situation. Being compassionate and empathetic to those around you can make the world a better place.

[5]
YOUR LAUGHTER
IS INFECTIOUS

Most people have heard the phrase "laughter is the best medicine." There is definitely truth to this because laughing has a positive impact on our health and well-being. When we laugh, our brain releases chemicals that make us feel happier and less stressed. These chemicals have been proven to improve physical health, emotional wellness, and even levels of creativity. You might notice when you see a funny meme or hear a good joke, you feel more alert and positive, especially if it makes you laugh. This encourages your mind and body to feel more open and confident.

Having infectious laughter means that when people hear you laugh, they feel those benefits too. Like your smile, your laugh can be contagious, brightening the days of those who hear it. Research shows that shared laughter is an important way for humans to socialize and connect. Laughter is found in all human social groups and cultures, and it's considered a fundamental part of communication and growth.

Not everyone will think that the same things are funny, and some things that you find funny now might not always make you laugh in the future. However, it's a good idea to look for something each day that brings you laughter. Some suggestions are remembering a funny situation, reading an entertaining story or comic, talking to your best friend, or watching a humorous video or movie.

Don't worry if you experience days when you don't feel like laughing because that's to be expected. There is nothing wrong with feeling down occasionally but knowing that your laughter is infectious and beneficial to others can make you appreciate the times when you do have a good laugh—and others around you will appreciate it as well.

[6]
YOU INSPIRE OTHERS

As we know, there is no one else quite like you. Because of this, you inspire others just by being yourself. When people feel inspired, they are motivated by something or someone to set, reach, and achieve goals. For example, you might be inspired by a performance of singing and dancing, which might lead you to set a goal to do something similar. This inspiration could result in you taking singing lessons or a dance class and maybe even performing in public to achieve your goal.

Sometimes, we get caught up in the way others are appreciated, which might inspire us to be more like them. This can be healthy in some ways, especially if you feel encouraged to try something new, improve certain skills, or pursue other productive outcomes. However, trying to be just like someone else simply for attention or appreciation from others is not genuine inspiration, and it can lead to unhealthy feelings and behaviors. It's far more inspiring to embrace being the best self you can be and let others be themselves.

Humans naturally look to others for inspiration. Usually, people think of artists, leaders, and hero figures (such as firefighters, doctors, and teachers) as inspiring. However, someone can inspire others in many ways that don't necessarily involve a certain talent, position, or level of bravery. You are likely an inspiration for many reasons, just by being you: your kindness, sense of humor, compassion, intelligence, and more. This is good to remember so that you can grow to appreciate your natural strengths and qualities and inspire others to do the same.

[7]
YOU ARE
RESILIENT

Resilience is the ability to recover from setbacks and persevere. This quality is important because it helps us to keep going despite mistakes, accidents, or unforeseen circumstances. Consider how toddlers learn to walk; they fall at an alarming rate, but their resilience allows them to get up and try again until they've mastered the steps.

Many people imagine a rubber band as an example of resilience because it can stretch quite a bit without breaking, and then it bounces back. Resilience in people is not about literally stretching and bouncing back, though. When people are resilient, it means that they can withstand situations that cause them difficulty without giving up.

You might not feel resilient in certain moments, especially if you are going through tough challenges. It's important in these situations to remember all the things you have overcome before and believe in your ability to keep going. Essential parts of resilience are patience and allowing yourself time to figure out the best way to bounce back. These traits will also help you learn your strengths and apply them to future situations, allowing you to become even more resolute and self-assured.

It's also important to remember that just because you are resilient doesn't mean that you can't ask for help or support. Knowing how to effectively use the resources available to you is part of being resilient; it means you don't have to feel all the responsibility on your shoulders. People are often inspired by groups and communities that have suffered losses and come together to improve their situations. Resilience is an excellent individual quality, but it's even stronger when people share and build resilience together.

[8]
YOUR CREATIVITY
KNOWS NO BOUNDS

Creativity is the quality that helps people use their imagination and come up with original ideas. Many people associate creativity with being artistic, having talents in such things as painting, sculpting, writing, and composing music. Though these are excellent ways to demonstrate creativity, there is no limit to how you can apply your creative nature.

Some of the most creative people in history include inventors, scientists, and even professional thinkers (often called philosophers) in addition to artists. These people typically have a lot in common, especially in allowing their imagination to thrive and grow. This means that they use their brains to come up with new ideas and concepts that go beyond what people experience in the natural world. Imagination and creative expression are unique to humans and a large part of what makes us interesting and unique.

No matter how you decide to use or express your creativity, it's important to nurture it. Daily life can become so busy that we often forget to let ourselves daydream and imagine. To nurture your creativity, allow yourself a little time each day for just thinking, wondering, and enjoying your imagination. This might lead you to remarkable ideas and new ways of expressing yourself simply by letting your mind wander.

[9]
YOU ALWAYS TRY TO SEE THE GOOD

One of the many reasons you're awesome is that you look for the good in situations. Sometimes, people describe this as "finding the silver lining," meaning that you approach even negative circumstances with the goal of finding something positive. This isn't always easy to do, but there are ways to develop a positive outlook to see the good in every situation.

Research shows that people who practice gratitude are often more likely to have an optimistic perspective. Practicing gratitude means taking a moment to feel thankful and appreciative of someone or something. This requires you to actively think of things to feel grateful for. For example, you might decide to express gratitude for a different person each night before you go to sleep. These can include family members, friends, teachers, coaches, and neighbors; just take a moment to feel thankful for their presence in your life.

Practicing gratitude can help you see the good in situations, and the more often you recognize and feel appreciation for both big and seemingly trivial things in the world, the more optimistic your perspective will be. This will allow you to see good, even in situations that might not look positive to others.

Sometimes, it can be difficult to see the good in a particular situation. This is especially true when events that we don't have any control over happen, such as illness or accidents. In those cases, it's understandable to feel negative, disappointed, and even sad. However, it's important to remember that life has a way of balancing positives and negatives, and it most likely won't be long before you are able to practice gratitude and see the good in situations again.

[10]
YOU'VE TOUCHED
COUNTLESS LIVES

Many of us go through each day without thinking much about the lives we touch. We interact with core groups of people nearly every day, such as our family, friends, classmates, and neighbors. We are aware of how we impact their lives and what we mean to those close to us. You might not always get along with your sibling or parents or best friend, but it's probably clear that you are significant and special in their lives.

You might be surprised to learn that you've impacted other people's lives, some that you might recognize as acquaintances and even some that you've never met. Every time you are friendly and kind to someone, you touch their life by making their day better. This could be anything from thanking the school bus driver to holding a door open for someone whose hands are full. Even sharing your smile with someone can make them feel better.

It might not be obvious how you touch the lives of people you've never met, but you very likely have. If you've ever donated clothing, toys, food, or other items to those less fortunate, you have made an impact on a stranger's life. This is also true if you've volunteered to better the community, recycled, or even thrown away a piece of litter that wasn't yours.

Sometimes, it's difficult to see or know that you have made a difference in the world. However, now that you understand the countless lives you've touched without even realizing it, you can feel encouraged that your presence in the world is valuable.

[11]
YOU'RE OPEN TO LEARNING NEW THINGS

Being open to learning new things is an awesome trait that can make life rewarding and exciting. Nearly two decades of our lives are spent in school or other formal educational environments, often absorbing what other people think is important to know. Depending on the circumstances, this can lead to frustration with learning and even a dislike for certain subjects. However, an openness to the learning journey can make even the most difficult or boring topic meaningful. If you have the right mindset, it can inspire you to be a lifelong learner.

Lifelong learners are self-motivated and appreciate exploring all types of knowledge. They approach learning new things as opportunities for personal growth, fun, and finding deeper meaning. This leads to different expectations than many people experience as students. Lifelong learners don't focus on an ideal grade or praise from an instructor; they pursue knowledge without feeling pressured to master the material or subjects. This approach allows people to keep an open mind, appreciating the learning process in addition to the chance to add to their knowledge.

The more open you are to learning new things, the more you will learn about yourself. As you explore different interests, you'll discover new things about yourself, other people, and the world. For example, you might try cooking and learn you have a talent for certain dishes that you love to share, or you might decide to learn a new language and then realize that traveling and exploring other cultures interests you. There are many opportunities to find what makes you feel passionate and fulfilled, and being open to learning will lead you to unexpected dreams, adventures, and ideas.

[12]
YOU SPREAD POSITIVITY WHEREVER YOU GO

Spreading positivity goes along with trying to see the good in each situation. Spreading positivity wherever you go doesn't mean that it's your responsibility to make everyone around you happy, though. That would be impossible! The positive impact you have on those around you has more to do with your outlook and how it affects and inspires others.

Most people keep a positive outlook by treating themselves with positivity. This means talking to yourself in an encouraging manner. Let's say, for example, you are disappointed with your grade on a test. The way you talk to yourself about it in your mind can determine whether you'll develop a positive or negative outlook. If you allow negative self-talk such as, "I'll never get a good grade in this class," or "I'm terrible at this subject," your outlook will likely be pessimistic. If you reassure yourself that it's just one test and there are options to improve in the future, your outlook will be much more positive.

Remember, having a positive outlook doesn't mean that you will only experience positive emotions. We all face stressful and negative situations, but your positivity can help you stay optimistic and not be derailed by setbacks. A positive outlook is formed by understanding that life is a balance between good and bad, and when you are a positive thinker, you spread that to others.

There are a lot of ways to share your positive outlook, from giving genuine compliments and encouragement to others to volunteering your time helping people and causes you believe in. You also spread positivity by just being who you are—a kind, compassionate, inspiring person.

[13]
YOUR KINDNESS CAN CHANGE SOMEONE'S DAY

Kindness is one of the most important attributes a person can have. It is the quality of treating others with respect, consideration, and generosity. Many people associate specific actions with kindness, such as helping less fortunate people, donating to charity, and so on. However, even small acts of kindness can change someone's day and make the world a better place.

For example, you might notice that your sibling is struggling with their homework and decide to offer them encouragement or a little help, or you might take a few minutes and set the table for dinner without being asked. These small acts of kindness will not only improve someone's day, but they can make you feel closer to your family as well. The more you practice kindness in your life, the more aware you'll be of the positive impact you are having.

Like smiling and laughter, kindness can be contagious. Most people greatly appreciate it when others are considerate and generous, and that appreciation is likely to inspire them to carry out acts of kindness in return. This often has a ripple effect that can positively impact many people's entire day and hopefully continue into the next one.

One thing to remember is to be kind to yourself too. We are often hard on ourselves through criticism and doubt in our self-talk (what we tell ourselves in our minds.) When we think and speak to ourselves with kindness, it can influence our brain patterns so that we grow to be more self-compassionate. So, not only can your kindness change someone else's day, but it can change your day when you apply it to yourself.

[14]
YOU ARE A GOOD LISTENER

Your ability to listen is exceptional. Listening is a powerful tool because it goes far beyond just hearing what someone says. When you actively listen to others, it shows that you are taking in their words by understanding and validating them. This improves communication by demonstrating interest and empathy toward the other person.

We often aren't aware of the things that can distract us from listening. We might be preoccupied or distracted with thoughts, phone notifications, or even the sights and sounds around us. However, it is rewarding to focus on what someone is saying with your ability to listen.

There are many benefits to being a good listener, no matter how old you are. Your ability to listen means you can build trust with others, avoid misunderstandings, and even create better friendships. Connecting with others is important for your mental and emotional well-being, and the simple act of listening is a huge part of building healthy, strong, and meaningful relationships.

In addition, the more you develop active listening skills, the more you'll grow as a leader and a learner. Active listening is when you give someone your full attention, process what they are saying, and then try to understand further by asking questions. This tells the person you are communicating with that you are fully invested in their thoughts and words, and it allows you to learn more about people, ideas, and diverse points of view. Active listening is also a characteristic of leadership, demonstrating that you are open to others.

Being an amazing listener doesn't mean you have to agree with everything a person says, though. It's important to stay true to yourself and your values. However, your amazing listening abilities will allow you to gain a deeper understanding of your friends, family members, teachers, and others, and that will help you grow as a person.

[15]
YOU CHAMPION
THE UNDERDOG

When people think of the word "underdog," they usually picture someone who is at a disadvantage or expected to lose in a competition or conflict. The underdog theme is especially popular in movies, as the audience is led to root for a character or group of characters who must overcome significant odds to succeed. This sometimes involves a story in which a team or player struggles for most of the plot and is triumphant at the end.

In the real world, underdogs might not be quite as easy to spot, and they might not always be able to overcome the obstacles in their path. That's why your ability to stand up for others is so special. It takes a great deal of empathy to recognize a situation where someone is an underdog and a lot of courage to support them and stand up for what is right.

For example, you might notice that someone is intentionally left out of a group because they are different in some way and decide to include them in your group. You might choose to volunteer your time with an organization that provides help to the less fortunate. Even small acts of support and kindness can make a big difference in someone's life, especially if that person faces disadvantages others don't.

Lots of circumstances in this world aren't fair. That's why when you champion the underdog and stand up for what's right, it makes you even more of an awesome person. Doing so shows you care about others and have the inner strength to be true to your values rather than just going along with a crowd or pretending not to notice when someone needs support.

[16]
YOU'RE
RESOURCEFUL

Knowing that you are capable and can make the best out of any situation can help you keep a positive outlook when things get challenging. This means you believe in your ability to discover ways to address challenges and that you have the perseverance to see things through.

Often, when people struggle with a problem or situation, their emotions affect the way they think. When we feel anxiety, fear, or sadness, it's hard not to be discouraged, which can lead to a negative outlook and expecting negative outcomes. In turn, this perspective interferes with our ability to find productive ways to address problems because we feel helpless. However, if we believe in our ability to persevere, discover alternate paths, and eventually find solutions, we have the power to see difficult situations in a better light.

Being resourceful means you can find creative and effective ways to overcome difficulties. This can help you make the best out of any situation. Resourceful people look for new and clever ways to solve problems or make an even bigger impact. Many resourceful people influence the world positively every day, such as scientists working to discover innovative medical treatments, teachers presenting lessons in new ways, and environmentalists figuring out better conservation techniques.

Your resourcefulness might lead to worldwide impacts someday, but even using your resourceful skills to navigate small, personal challenges makes a difference. The more you recognize how resourceful you are, the better you will be at making the best out of any situation.

[17]
YOU HAVE A WEALTH OF KNOWLEDGE

Many people think of knowledge as what we learn in school. That's true, but academic education isn't the only source of what we can learn. There are many types of knowledge and expertise, and you might be surprised how much you know and what you can share with others.

Outside of what we learn in a classroom—which is important— our overall knowledge of the world comes from many sources. For example, you know a great deal about where you live, how to perform daily tasks, and how to communicate. You also have expertise when it comes to your family and culture. Your family might celebrate certain holidays or traditions that others don't. This is just part of the wealth of knowledge you have to share.

Our hobbies and interests also provide us with an abundance of knowledge. You might be an expert when it comes to a certain video game or sport. If you like reading and writing, you probably know a lot about literary genres and maybe some influential authors. People who play a musical instrument or take singing lessons know about music as an art form. There really is no end to the knowledge we can accumulate just by pursuing our creativity and passion. When we share that with others, they might develop the same interests as well.

It's important to remember that what you know and how much you know is more significant when it means something to you. So, be sure to expand your sources of knowledge and be open to opportunities. This will help you become a lifelong learner and add to the wealth of knowledge you already have that you can share with others.

[18]
YOU HAVE
BIG DREAMS

One of the things that makes you an awesome individual is your dreams. When you have big, bold, and beautiful dreams, it means you embrace your imagination, have confidence in yourself to be daring, and possess the energy to strive for your goals.

When most people hear the word "dream," they think of the experience that happens during sleep. In this case, however, the focus is on your conscious dreams. This can be anything from letting your mind wander and explore possibilities to imagining what you want for your future. When we dream in a big, bold way, it motivates us toward success, as if we can "see" our potential ambitions and accomplishments.

Some of the most notable people, current and historical, are dreamers. They envision a future unlike anyone else and then work to find ways to make their dream a reality. This has led to innovations in science, medicine, environmentalism, technology, and even art. One way to realize your dreams in the future is to describe them in a journal. That way, you can revisit and expand on your thoughts and ideas.

Even if your dreams seem too big or complex, they can inspire you to consider your options and work toward smaller goals as a way of making progress. The beauty of your dreams is that they are unique to you, drive your successes, and keep your sense of wonder alive.

[19]
YOU CAN SEE BEAUTY IN THE SIMPLE THINGS

Seeing beauty in the simplest things means that you take the time to notice how remarkable and lovely the world can be, just as it is. Our schedules tend to be so busy that it can seem impossible to look around and appreciate the simple beauty of things like flowers, raindrops, and squirrels running around. There is beauty to be seen outside nature as well; you might notice a simple gesture, a smile, or even the way your bed looks when you make it, which can also be beautiful.

Sometimes, it's difficult to avoid getting caught up in certain beauty standards, especially when it comes to fashion, technology, and outward appearance. There is so much clever marketing out there for products that not only promise to make us more beautiful as individuals but our lives more beautiful as well. Advertisers know how to influence our insecurities about belonging and having the "right" brand or latest upgrade. This can lead to negative outcomes, from unnecessary spending to struggles with body image. It also sets up a cycle of high expectations and results that often fall short.

That's why being able to see beauty in the simplest things is such an incredible strength. It keeps you grounded in the moment and grateful for what is present around you. Remember to see the beauty in the simple things about yourself as well, from the light in your eyes to the color of your skin.

[20]
YOU'RE PASSIONATE

Humans have all kinds of belief systems. These might be based on things like faith, religion, politics, social justice, or education. When people are passionate about what they believe in, they feel connected to something larger than themselves. For example, you might have a strong belief in being environmentally conscious as a means of protecting the Earth and its inhabitants. This environmental passion might lead you to participate in activities that impact more than just your life, such as creating an urban garden and green space. You are also more likely to support environmental friendliness on an individual level, such as reducing energy usage, opting for plastic-free goods, and making efforts to recycle.

As passionate as you are about what you believe, it's important to remember to keep an open mind. Our beliefs can change over time as we gather knowledge and experience. Just as you wouldn't expect your clothes to get bigger as you do, you should expect that some beliefs won't grow along with you or be an exact fit in the future. This is a good thing because it allows us to adapt to new information and develop different perspectives.

It's also important to be respectful of others' beliefs. Even if they don't align with yours, others likely feel as passionate about what they believe as you do. Strong beliefs help people feel connected, inspired, and valued, so allow yourself to feel passionate about what you believe and support others in their process as well.

[21]
YOU'VE MADE SACRIFICES FOR OTHERS

The word "sacrifice" is traditionally applied to acts found in mythology and religion. A more real-world definition of sacrifice is the act of giving up something valuable to you as a way of helping or benefiting someone else. Making a sacrifice in this way is usually perceived as selfless, generous, charitable, and compassionate.

For example, you might want to spend your Saturday sleeping in, playing video games, and relaxing with friends—all of which are excellent weekend activities. However, you might be asked to sacrifice those personal interests for activities that benefit others, such as helping with household chores, visiting your grandparents, or babysitting a younger sibling. Sometimes, we make sacrifices for others without being asked, like giving our time to volunteer for a community clean-up, helping a neighbor shovel their walkway in winter, or even taking an extra minute to gather stray shopping carts in a parking lot.

Most of the time, we feel good about sacrificing our time and energy for a productive cause or valuable reason. However, it's important to remember that making certain sacrifices for others can have negative outcomes. This is especially true if you are asked or decide to do something on behalf of someone else that causes harm to your physical health, emotional stability, or mental well-being. If you are facing this type of situation, it's essential to seek help and guidance from a reliable loved one or respected professional. It's fine to make some mutually beneficial sacrifices, but it's never okay to compromise your health or safety.

[22]
YOUR INTUITION
GUIDES YOU

You might notice that you have a strong feeling about something sometimes, whether it's a person, a school subject, or even a job opportunity. This feeling comes from your intuition and often helps guide you in making choices and decisions. People who trust their intuition generally report successful experiences and even less overall anxiety. Being mindful of what our intuition tells us is also an effective way of eliminating the pressures of other people's opinions, suggestions, and demands, some of which might not lead to the best outcomes.

Your intuition is a bit like an inner voice that might lead you in a particular direction. Intuition comes from knowing something through instinct and feeling rather than active thought or reason. For example, you might be interested in joining a new club at the start of the school year, and your intuition might guide you when it comes to narrowing your choices. In other words, you might just have a feeling that you'd prefer to be part of a group that focuses more on academics than athletics or one that meets in the morning as opposed to after school.

There are times when you might not experience any intuition about a situation, and this is to be expected. However, as you grow in your experiences and learning, you will likely recognize when your instincts are trying to lead you.

Our intuition can be an amazing and helpful guide, but it shouldn't become a substitute for critical thinking. This is especially true when it comes to big or important decisions. That's why it's important to balance your instincts with rational thought. This way, your intuition will continue to guide you in amazing ways.

[23]
YOUR ENERGY
IS MAGNETIC

When someone's energy is magnetic, others are drawn to the spirit and passion of who they are. Positive energy reflects enthusiasm and liveliness, which is welcoming to people. This energy helps you achieve your goals and make the world a better place.

Everyone needs time to recharge their energy. This might mean taking quiet moments to read or rest so your well-being is restored. We are often caught up in the busy activities of our daily lives, so we might forget to allow ourselves the opportunity to relax. This can deplete our natural energy so that we turn to less desirable behaviors like consuming things like caffeine and sugar to maintain productivity. This can not only create a vicious cycle of ups and downs, but it might drain your energy even further.

Therefore, it's important to remember to check in with yourself and gauge your energy levels. If you notice that you are feeling burnout or less enthusiasm for things you usually enjoy, take some time to focus on yourself and reduce your stress. There are many ways to revitalize your energy, such as taking a walk, visiting a friend, listening to music, or watching a movie. When you maintain a balance in your life, you'll feel healthier, and your energy will be even more magnetic.

[24]
YOU'RE HONEST AND GENUINE

Many people assume that the words "honest" and "genuine" mean the same thing, but there is a subtle difference. A genuine person is authentic and sincere, meaning that their words and actions reflect their true thoughts and intentions. An honest person is truthful and rarely intends to deceive others with their words or actions.

As an honest and genuine person, other people see you as reliable and trustworthy. These are important character traits at any age, and they are especially appreciated in friendships, the workplace, and society as a whole. Of course, nobody is perfect; at times, you might find yourself exaggerating or acting in a way that is out of character to fit in with a group. These instances shouldn't worry you as long as you consistently work to be true to yourself and others.

There are certain situations in which it might feel difficult to be completely honest or genuine. For example, if your friend asks what you think of their sweater and it's just not your style, you wouldn't want your honesty to hurt their feelings. In cases like this, you can rely on what is known as "tact." Tact is the ability to handle situations with sensitivity and thoughtfulness toward others. In terms of your friend's sweater, you can be honest with tact by telling them that their sweater looks good on them or that you're happy they're expressing themselves.

As you grow, you will value and appreciate honest and genuine people — including yourself. This is just another reason you are an awesome individual.

[25]
YOU DARE TO PURSUE YOUR DREAMS

When we allow ourselves to dream, it strengthens our imagination and encourages us to consider possibilities. This develops our creativity and leads to a desire to achieve amazing things. When you dare to dream, you can discover even more about yourself. Earlier, we talked about how our unique dreams are special, but what makes you really awesome is your ability to pursue those dreams and work toward making them a reality.

Pursuing your dreams is one of the most rewarding aspects of life. One of the best ways to successfully pursue your dreams is to imagine an end goal and then create a plan to get there. Most people find it helpful to create small steps within an overall plan to help you make progress and stay on track to fulfilling your goals. This also allows you to be flexible, as our dreams and goals often change over time and with experience.

For example, you might dream of running a marathon. Rather than signing up for one and hoping you make it through, it's wiser to set up small steps that help you train safely and properly condition for such a long race. As you develop your skills, you might find that you enjoy sprinting more than distance running, so allowing yourself to be flexible with your dream might lead you to something different than the marathon you originally planned.

It's also fine to just appreciate certain dreams as they are. For example, you might daydream about what you would do if you won the lottery, became famous, or had the power of invisibility. These dreams aren't necessarily intended to turn into goals; they are more a way of keeping our imagination active and allowing our creativity an outlet. The important thing to remember is that it's healthy and fun to dare to dream and pursue those dreams to the best of your ability.

[26]
YOU MAKE THE ORDINARY EXTRAORDINARY

When something is described as "extraordinary," that means it is remarkable or exceptional. People tend to use this word in reference to amazing athletes, performers, leaders, or even food and art. Anything that goes beyond the ordinary can be considered extraordinary. Turning something ordinary into something extraordinary is a way of embracing the goodness and wonder of the world in which we live.

It's often difficult to notice what is special about the ordinary parts of our lives because we are so familiar with them that they fade into the background. For example, your route to school or work might seem so ordinary to you that it becomes routine or even tedious. Yet, if you take a moment to notice small details, such as how the season has changed, your fellow commuters, or the unique aspects of where you live, your ordinary route can seem extraordinary.

When people are around you, they notice your energy, perspective, and what you appreciate in the world. This can make what would otherwise be ordinary appear extraordinary to them. Viewing your environment and the people around you through a lens that allows you to notice wonderful details is an extraordinary characteristic and a big part of what makes you awesome.

[27]
YOU HAVE A GRATEFUL MINDSET

Gratitude is a rewarding and valuable human trait. As we practice gratitude, we develop empathy for others and an appreciation for the world around us. Allowing our hearts to feel thankful is also beneficial in terms of physical, emotional, and mental well-being. This is partly why so many people are fond of Thanksgiving and other holidays that remind us of our blessings.

There are many ways to actively feel gratitude every day. Some people keep journals and make lists of why they are thankful. Others begin or end the day by thinking of three—or more—

specific people, events, feelings, or whatever makes them feel grateful. This can be as simple as recognizing your appreciation for nice weather or receiving a smile from someone you don't know. Most people who purposely incorporate feeling thankful in their everyday lives find that they see even more reasons to have a heart full of gratitude, just like yours.

Actively feeling gratitude can encourage you not only to be more thankful but more hopeful as well. Sometimes, it's difficult to remember that there is a lot of good in people and the world, especially during challenging times. When we consciously think about what we are grateful for, it provides us with reassurance, peace, and hope.

There are external ways of expressing the gratitude that you feel on the inside as well. Writing a thank-you note, sending an appreciative text, or even just giving an unexpected hug to someone you love are all healthy ways of showing your gratitude and what's in your heart. Who knows? Those actions might just end up on someone else's thankful list!

[28]
YOU NEVER
STOP TRYING

When you never stop trying, no matter how difficult things get, you show perseverance. This means that you continue doing something meaningful despite challenges, delays, or setbacks. Perseverant people tend to not only achieve their goals but also learn and grow a great deal along the way.

Perseverance comes in many forms, such as not giving up, using creative thinking to address problems, and focusing on the achievement of small steps to reach a goal. This character trait helps you develop resilience and focus so you can accomplish what is important to you. Often, when we want to achieve something meaningful, there are obstacles along the path to success. When you keep trying, even if things get hard, you will likely find a way to succeed and become physically, mentally, and emotionally stronger in the process.

There are certain situations in which we are truly limited. Under those circumstances, a way to keep trying is to alter the desired outcome. For example, if you are too young to compete at the varsity level on an athletic team, you can change your goal to becoming a leader at the junior varsity level. As you keep persevering, once you meet the team's age requirement, you will likely be rewarded and appreciated for your hard work. You'll also have the confidence to meet future challenges and not let them discourage you from trying.

[29]
YOUR STORIES ARE A TESTAMENT OF YOUR JOURNEY

You already know that you are a unique individual and that there is nobody just like you. Part of what makes you different from everyone else is what you've experienced. Your experiences become stories that make up your journey through life.

Your stories and experiences serve as evidence of what you have been through and what it means to you. Everyone travels through life on a different path, and they interpret what happens to them in individual ways. For example, what might seem like an obstacle to one person might be interpreted by another as a welcome challenge. However, though each person makes their own journey, we share our stories with others along the way. Therefore, our journey is not an isolated one but a path that interacts and intersects with all kinds of people.

Ultimately, you have the power to embrace your experiences and create stories to help you define who you are. Some experiences will be more significant than others, and you might even forget certain stories over time. However, it's important to remember that your path is not set in stone; your experiences and stories have meaning, and your life's journey belongs to you.

[30]
YOU CHERISH
YOUR RELATIONSHIPS

You have many relationships to value and cherish—some might even surprise you! Most of the time, we think of family and friends when we consider the people who are important to us. However, you have other people and relationships in your life that contribute to your learning, joy, and overall well-being, and these should be valued and cherished as well.

Consider the people you interact with frequently, even daily. These might include teachers, coaches, counselors, or neighbors. All these relationships impact your life, some for the short term and others for life. You might also have relationships with people you've never met, perhaps through playing video games, online clubs, or other virtual groups. These are additional relationships you might appreciate and hold dear.

When we value and cherish a relationship, we treat the other person with respect, kindness, and generosity. One important relationship that you might not have considered is the relationship you have with yourself. It might sound strange at first, but the way you treat yourself can influence your health and well-being, as well as your relationships with other people.

Therefore, it's essential to treat yourself with respect, kindness, and generosity. For example, if you notice that you are being critical of yourself, try to imagine that you are encouraging a friend instead and change your self-talk. Your relationship with yourself will last a lifetime, and it should be valued and cherished just as much as any other relationship.

[31]
YOUR SENSE OF HUMOR
LIFTS OTHERS' SPIRITS

As you know, laughter can be contagious, and your sense of humor has the power to lift people's spirits. This doesn't mean that you have to make people laugh each day for them to appreciate and benefit from your sense of humor, though. It's much more about your approach to the quirks of daily life and being able to find some playfulness or positivity in response.

Some of us might think of comedy when we hear the word "humor." However, a person's sense of humor is not just the ability to tell or appreciate a good joke. It's a healthy way of looking at the world and not taking everything too seriously. For example, you might get dressed in such a hurry one morning that you put on mismatched socks. Having a sense of humor in this situation would help you not feel embarrassed or let it negatively affect your day.

Your sense of humor can also lift other people's spirits by encouraging them to feel more positive and lighthearted if the situation allows. Of course, there are times and circumstances in which humor is not appropriate, and it's important to show consideration in those moments. In addition, not everyone will find the same things to be funny, but that doesn't mean a sense of humor can't be shared. Overall, your sense of humor reflects an appropriately joyful attitude and cheerful outlook that can inspire others to feel the same.

[32]
YOU'RE
SOMEONE'S HERO

Just as you have touched the lives of others and inspired people without knowing it, you might be surprised to learn you are someone's hero. This doesn't mean they believe you spend half your time fighting crime or going into battle, but rather that you have heroic qualities. For example, you might have a sibling, neighbor, or school friend who looks up to you and admires your strength, leadership skills, and integrity.

A hero isn't necessarily someone who commits an act of bravery or prevents a disaster. Heroes are often everyday people who inspire others through their generosity, honesty, and dedication. It's important to consider your heroes or people you admire. They are most likely people you know and look up to for who they are. Your hero might be a member of your family, a teacher, a coach, or a neighbor. Chances are, they don't even know you consider them a hero.

It might seem uncomfortable to you at first that someone would find you heroic, but you don't need to make any big changes (like wearing a cape.) You have many qualities to admire that are part of your natural personality. As long as you continue to be kind, generous, dedicated, and honest toward others, you'll have earned the hero title.

[33]
YOU GIVE MORE
THAN YOU TAKE

A giving nature is one of the most admirable human characteristics. Most people associate the quality of giving with generosity and charity, which are important elements of this trait. However, being a giving person doesn't always mean offering something material like money or gifts. You can give in many ways without providing something tangible. These include volunteering your time, offering your support, and being an active listener.

Though it's rewarding and commendable to be a giver rather than a taker, it's also essential to set healthy limits. In other words, your giving nature should make you feel balanced and productive rather than drained and resentful. Unfortunately, some people choose to take advantage of the kindness and generosity of others. If you find yourself in a position where someone is treating you unfairly or imposing on your selfless personality in an uncomfortable way, it's wise to set boundaries to protect yourself.

As you learn and grow, you will find a sense of value and peace in giving more than you take. This mindset tends to be reciprocal, meaning that you are likely to be appreciated for your efforts and supported in return. Not everyone will have the same resources, abilities, or tendencies, but the more you can give to others in a healthy way, the more rewarded you will feel.

[34]
YOUR PERSPECTIVE
IS REFRESHING

"Perspective" refers to your point of view about something or your attitude toward it. Everyone has a unique perspective, which is helpful when it comes to creativity, problem-solving, and empathy. Learning other people's perspectives can give you a much better understanding of the big picture and the way others see it.

As we get older and gain experience and knowledge, our perspectives can change. When you were a child, you might have had a negative perspective regarding a set bedtime. Most children prefer to stay up later than they should, but parents typically set a bedtime so they can get enough rest. You might have thought your bedtime was unfair or illogical; however, as you get older, become busier, and have to get up earlier for school or work, your perspective regarding a set bedtime might change. You are more likely to set one for yourself and welcome it so you can get enough sleep to maintain your health and well-being.

Your perspective is refreshing and enlightening because it is unique. It is influenced by your experiences but also by your thoughtfulness, originality, and empathy. As you develop and share your perspective, you allow others to see a different point of view, and your openness will encourage people to share their perspectives, which can give you new insight and understanding.

[35]
YOU'RE CONSTANTLY EVOLVING

Though it might be hard to notice in the present moment, you are constantly evolving and improving. It's easier to recognize your progress if you look back at who you were and compare that to your current self. You will likely realize how much you've grown, matured, and learned through your experiences. This will encourage you to keep improving so that who you become in the future is even more special.

Evolving as a person means that you encourage yourself to learn, grow, and adapt. This is important because as we are introduced to new ideas, people, and experiences, we tend to change our thought patterns and perspectives. It's essential to remain flexible so you can evolve into the strongest, wisest, and kindest person possible.

Improving as a person means that you take opportunities to enrich who you are. You might realize that time management is something of a challenge for you. To improve your daily organization and punctuality, you might decide to research suggestions to better manage your time. You might even consult people you admire for tips on time management. Then, you can implement the strategies that work for you and appreciate the improvements you've made.

You should assess yourself regularly to figure out how you can evolve or where you can improve. It's important to remember that you are naturally awesome for being yourself to begin with and that you will stay flexible and recognize improvement opportunities when they appear.

[36]
YOU FACE YOUR FEARS HEAD-ON

It's part of human nature to ignore, deny, or hide from our fears. Fear is a difficult emotion that can cause a wide range of physical and mental responses. This includes everything from rapid breathing and heart rate to anxiety and negative thoughts. For these and many other reasons, the natural behavior of humans is to avoid their fears.

It might be surprising to learn that certain fears are healthy and keep us from harm. It's natural to feel fear when we encounter dangerous situations, environments, or experiences. This is part of our survival instinct as a species. However, some fears can reach an unhealthy level and negatively affect our quality of life.

For example, public speaking is one of the most common fears among people. Just the idea of speaking in public can create nervousness, stress, and worry for those with this fear. Thankfully, it's possible to overcome a fear of public speaking once you are aware of this response. Mindfulness, preparation, practice, and studying other public speakers are some of the techniques people use to face this fear.

There are some excellent general strategies to help you face your specific fears head-on. It's best to approach overcoming your anxiety by acknowledging what causes it and taking small steps to address it. These steps might include talking through your emotions, practicing calming breathing techniques, and even allowing yourself limited exposure to what you fear until you feel more at ease. It's important to never judge yourself—or others—for experiencing this emotion, no matter how silly your fears might seem. Compassion for yourself and others in fearful situations will give you the strength to face and eventually overcome your fears.

[37]
YOU HAVE A
ZEST FOR LIFE

When people use the phrase "zest for life," they typically mean an attitude that shows a general excitement and positivity toward people and the world. Individuals who have a zest for life enjoy the moment, appreciate new experiences, and are willing to embrace things as they are and find the good in them.

Your zest for life is infectious, meaning that the people around you notice this attitude, and it fills them with the same feeling and outlook. Most children have a zest for life, as shown by their adventurous spirit, humor, and curiosity. Unfortunately, as people get older, they sometimes let negativity overshadow their childlike excitement and open-mindedness. This is to be expected, especially when life becomes challenging and hardships are faced.

However, if you can maintain a zest for life most of the time, you're likely to appreciate the little moments that come your way, as well as big life events. This attitude is sure to inspire others to approach life in the same way, as much as possible.

[38]
YOUR PASSION
IS PALPABLE

If a feeling or idea is "palpable," that means that it is so strong you can almost touch it. A good example of something palpable would be the excitement of an upcoming holiday or the strong sense of anticipation for a celebration. It's not something that can be physically touched, but the signs of what is upcoming are hard to miss, whether in the form of decorations, music, food, or the way people behave.

Your passion is palpable in the same way. When you feel excitement and dedication toward something, you exude that passion so strongly that others can feel it as well. This is an inspiring trait, even if others don't share your exact passion. For example, you might be passionate about dramatic arts. You might display this passion by volunteering or acting in a community theater, attending live productions, and encouraging others to enjoy performances. Though some of your friends and family members might not share your excitement for the dramatic arts, they can recognize and appreciate your passion for it. This might even encourage them to become more interested in the art form.

Your palpable passions also allow others to get to know you and develop connections. Shared interests are an excellent way to meet new people and establish friendships. Your passions might change over time as you grow in your knowledge and experiences, which is healthy. No matter what inspires your passion, make sure you let it shine so it's palpable to others.

[39]
YOU LEARN FROM YOUR MISTAKES

Mistakes are part of being human. They represent inevitable errors or lapses in judgment, and thankfully, most mistakes are minor enough to cause short-term inconveniences rather than long-term impacts. Repeating our mistakes, however, can hinder our success in relationships, school, work, and even achieving peace of mind. That's why it's so important that you learn from your mistakes and grow from them.

Sometimes, it's difficult to look at our mistakes and identify what we can learn from them, especially if they are embarrassing or discouraging. However, when we review what went wrong, we can use our mistakes as an opportunity to grow and avoid similar situations in the future. For example, if you have been late to school or work more than once due to indecision about what to wear, it's important to look at the mistakes that might have led to this problem. Perhaps you haven't kept up with your laundry, or you wait until the last minute to check the weather before you get dressed. When you confront your mistakes, you can change your behavior to achieve better outcomes. This helps you learn and grow as a person.

Some mistakes are minor slip-ups or tiny accidents, such as selecting "pm" rather than "am" for your alarm or getting part of an eggshell in cookie batter. These mistakes are common—and hopefully rare enough that you don't need to take life lessons from them. It's also important to remember not to dwell on your mistakes by rehashing them over and over in your mind or continuing to analyze them in detail. The best way to grow from your mistakes is to learn what you can and then move on so you can apply your learning in the future if necessary.

[40]
YOU FIND TIME
FOR YOUR LOVED ONES

It might surprise you to learn that what most people want from their loved ones is their time. This means that spending quality time with the ones you love is one of the most valuable things you can contribute to your relationships. Quality time is not based on the number of hours you spend with someone; it's the level of care you put into the time that matters. This might include being present in the moment through active listening, sharing your thoughts, or even just being there to hold a hand or give a hug.

When you find time for the ones you love, it shows commitment to your significant relationships. It can be difficult to step away from our busy schedules or even notice when someone might need our support. One way to avoid getting too wrapped up in our lives is to check in with loved ones regularly. This can be a simple text or phone call to show that they are in your thoughts. These small gestures will let others know how much they mean to you and that you are there for them.

Finding time for the ones you love also means finding time for yourself. This is especially important because taking time for yourself allows you to recharge so that you are at your best for others as well. Some people enjoy taking time for hobbies such as art, music, or gaming. For others, the chance to recharge might include reading a book, talking with friends, or going for a walk. No matter what activity you choose to de-stress and prioritize yourself, be sure you find the time each day to show yourself some love.

[41]
YOU MAKE OTHERS FEEL VALUED

One of your most awesome qualities is the way you make others feel valued and important. People who are appreciative, giving, and considerate in this way often feel more secure and confident in their value and wish to share that feeling with others. Most of us interact with a surprising number of strangers, acquaintances, and people we know well each day. However, our busy schedules and hurried pace can interfere with the way we demonstrate and reflect the value and importance that others have in our lives.

We might assume that our family, friends, and other close loved ones realize how valued and important they are to us. However, it's helpful to remind them occasionally of the appreciation and love we feel. To do this, you might send them a nice text, write a thank-you note, or even take care of a small favor without being asked. The smallest gestures can add up when it comes to making our loved ones feel special and cherished.

It's also wonderful to make others outside our family and social circles feel important and valued. Again, small gestures that reflect appreciation and kindness can have a big impact on the way we make others feel. For example, making eye contact and saying a genuine thank you to a service worker can show you value their effort. Holding a door open or allowing someone to go ahead of you in line are other gestures that indicate you are aware of and considerate toward other people.

[42]
YOU'RE CONSTANTLY SEEKING KNOWLEDGE

As a lifelong learner, you know how important it is to continually seek knowledge. Gaining knowledge and experience and being open to learning new things is how we develop wisdom as well.

Wisdom is what helps us put our knowledge to use by allowing us to exercise sound judgment and good sense.

In many ways, knowledge—or at least information—is easier to access than ever before. Most of the topics we wonder about or want to know can be researched online. There are also other sources of knowledge, such as educational instructors, coaches, parents, books, and even podcasts. However, it's one thing to look something up or temporarily memorize a fact or formula for an exam, but quite another to internalize what we learn so the knowledge stays with us and grows. The best way to do this is by being an active learner, which means thinking about the knowledge you have gained, considering how to apply it, and building on it for future learning.

Active learners not only internalize knowledge, but they also seek and build wisdom by making connections and finding meaning in their experiences. For example, you might be studying higher-level math with theories and principles that don't seem relevant to your future. However, if you internalize the experience and knowledge of problem-solving in math, that process might benefit you in other subjects, such as science. As you build practical experience, knowledge, and wisdom, you might be surprised to find that your learning serves many purposes. This will be a powerful reward for the knowledge and wisdom you are constantly seeking.

[43]
YOU CHERISH
THE LITTLE MOMENTS

We capture many big life events, such as birthdays, graduations, weddings, and holidays, through videos, photos, and personal memories. However, many little moments that we might not take the time to appreciate and cherish are just as special. This might be due to our busy schedules, preoccupied thoughts, or other interruptions. However, understanding how to hold these small instances dear is a way to preserve them in our memories, along with more significant events.

Some examples of little moments to cherish would be the way your pet greets you as you come home, the first sign of a new season approaching, or enjoying game night with your family. One way to capture these moments is to take time to reflect each day. You might do this by practicing active gratitude each morning or evening, keeping in mind little moments of the day as well as big ones. You might even set an alarm for a random point in your day to remind yourself to notice and admire the world around you. No matter how we approach it, cherishing the little moments that take place in our lives requires us to be present and mindful so we can appreciate them when they happen and remember them long afterward.

[44]
YOU MAKE
A DIFFERENCE

If you pause to consider all the people who have made a difference in your life, you might be surprised by the number of examples that come to mind. You might also be surprised to find how many people feel you have made a difference in their lives as well.

There are many ways to make a difference in someone's life. Sometimes, that difference is obvious, such as a parent keeping you safe, a friend making you laugh when you are sad, or a coach inspiring you to reach your full potential. There are also many people who make subtle differences in your life. For example, you might have an especially attentive dentist who ensures that your oral health is top-notch, or there might be a distant relative who never forgets to send you holiday greetings. Your actions, big and small, make a difference to the people in your life and impact them in positive ways.

You also likely contribute in meaningful ways to the lives of people you might not know. When we volunteer our time, make charitable donations, or participate in community activities, it can make a big difference to those who have disadvantages. Even our everyday behaviors can have a positive impact on others in the way we smile at people, show them courtesy, and express our appreciation. Knowing that you make a difference can feel rewarding and inspire you to do even more to improve the world around you.

[45]
YOUR DETERMINATION
IS COMMENDABLE

"Determination" refers to someone's sense of purpose and their commitment to following through. A famous folk tale published nearly a century ago called *The Little Engine That Could* by Watty Piper tells the story of a little train that helps bring toys and treats over a mountain. The train shows determination in climbing the mountain and fulfilling its purpose, repeating the phrase, "I think I can." This story captures the traits that make up determination, such as belief in oneself, positive thinking, setting clear goals, and perseverance.

Just like the little engine in the tale, your determination is commendable, meaning your focus and hard work are admirable and praiseworthy. This includes all the goals you have set and worked to achieve. It's also important to know that your determination counts even if it goes without notice or praise. Though it's nice to receive acknowledgment and praise, your internal validation of your perseverance and sense of purpose is what will help your determination and belief in yourself continue to grow. This means that you don't have to wait for someone else to commend your determination. Instead, you can reinforce this characteristic by taking pride in and appreciating yourself.

Everyone gets discouraged, though, and this can undermine your determination and seem difficult to overcome. However, these times are also opportunities for you to rediscover your belief in yourself and develop your positive thinking. The more you persevere, the more evidence you have that your determination is strong, worthwhile, and absolutely commendable.

[46]
YOU RECOGNIZE OTHERS' ACHIEVEMENTS

In many ways, we live in a competitive and achievement-focused society. This can be beneficial in that it might inspire people to work toward success and be rewarded for achieving it. However, it can also focus our attention on our ambitions and goals so much that we become unaware of what others are accomplishing. That's why it's so special that you not only recognize the achievements of others but that you celebrate them as well.

Competition can be healthy; it encourages people to work hard, come up with innovative ideas, and develop problem-solving skills. The downside to an excessive or unhealthy sense of competition is the lack of support and appreciation for other competitors. Some people might feel that acknowledging or admiring the success of others would undermine their own accomplishments, but that's far from true. Not only does it demonstrate good sportsmanship to congratulate others on their achievements, but it also reflects your individual strength and self-confidence.

When you recognize and celebrate others' achievements, you reveal your thoughtful and generous spirit. You understand that others' accomplishments do not diminish your achievements, and allowing yourself to honor other people's successes can feel just as rewarding as achieving your goals and dreams.

[47]
YOU FIND JOY
IN GIVING

Most people have heard the phrase, "It is better to give than to receive." This is usually said in a gift-giving context, around birthdays or Christmas, and it's often directed at children to remind them to be less concerned with what they get than what they give. Receiving a gift or a surprise can be lovely. However, you are awesome enough to know that there is great joy in giving to others.

People might judge the quality of what they give by how much it costs or the time and effort that are put into it. Of course, there is joy in giving material gifts and doing big favors for people. However, you have the capacity to give in other ways that reflect just as much quality and that will bring joy to you as well as others. Just the small act of giving someone a smile or a genuine compliment can brighten their day and yours — and it's free! You can also give by volunteering your time, being attentive to someone you care about, and working to make your community a better place.

The reward for having a generous, joyful, and giving spirit is understanding that you make a difference in the lives of people around you. People are far more likely to remember how special you make them feel than anything money can buy.

[48]
YOU'RE AUTHENTIC
AND REAL

We've already established that you are an honest and genuine person. In addition to that, you are authentic and real. This means that you don't feel the need to be or act like anyone other than yourself.

Sometimes, it can feel awkward or uncomfortable to be our authentic selves. This is especially true if you sense or assume that your interests, personality traits, or other aspects are extremely different from others around you. Fortunately, this is likely a misguided perception. Most people are much more critical of themselves than they are of others, and humans are far more alike than not. Yet, if you don't feel as though you quite fit in with certain groups or environments, take heart in the knowledge that you'll eventually find people who will love and accept you for exactly who you are.

One way to appreciate and reinforce the way you are authentic and real is to seek out others who share your passions. This might involve joining a gaming community online, taking a class at a community center, or even starting a group like a book club or something similar. Another way to express your authenticity is to offer encouragement to and admiration for other people you know who are comfortable being real in front of the world. It takes courage to be authentic and show your individuality, but there's nothing more rewarding than knowing that you are true to your real self.

[49]
YOU RADIATE WARMTH AND LOVE

Warmth and love come in many forms, and most people gravitate toward people—like you—who radiate these qualities. In this case, to "radiate" means to emit light or spread energy like the sun and stars. Part of the warmth and love you radiate is reflected in your generous nature, caring attitude, and sincere smile. When you open your heart and mind to others, it encourages them to be open with you as well. Treating people with compassion builds empathy and understanding, which can strengthen the warmth and love that people express and feel in their relationships.

It's understandable to have days when you don't feel like radiating warmth and love. One idea to keep in mind at such times is that you deserve warmth and love from yourself. Giving yourself love might come in the form of a relaxing activity such as taking a bath, reading a book, or listening to your favorite music. You can also practice self-love and compassion by choosing healthy habits such as regular exercise, a nutritious diet, and quality sleep. Allowing yourself to recharge when you need to experience warmth and love is essential to your long-term well-being. Before you know it, you'll be back to radiating warmth and love, both inside and out.

[50]
YOU TRUST
THE JOURNEY

You know that the journey of your life is not a straight line of ordered events. Most of us will imagine our future in a very different way than it will turn out. This is often because of opportunities and circumstances we can't foresee, in addition to the way our minds, goals, and dreams change over time. Being able to trust your path, no matter what detours or obstacles you encounter, can enhance your happiness and well-being. A big part of that is learning to go with the flow in potentially frustrating moments while keeping your overall journey in mind.

To "go with the flow" means that, in certain circumstances, you allow yourself to accept things as they are without resisting or trying to change them. For example, you might expect that it will take you an hour to run some easy errands, but then you experience a traffic delay, or a store might be out of what you need. Rather than feeling angry or defeated, if you let yourself go with the flow, you'll find the patience to accept the situation and not let it cause you stress that can hinder your path.

When you trust your journey and embrace flexibility, you will become much more resilient in the face of challenges and more open to new opportunities that come your way. In addition, your acceptance and peace of mind will allow you to navigate your path so that you have a clear vision of happiness and success. This includes being adaptable in setting your goals and planning the steps to achieve them.

[51]
YOU BELIEVE IN
LOVE AND KINDNESS

Sometimes, the world can feel discouraging, especially when we focus on the injustices many people face and the overwhelming challenges that seem impossible to overcome. One of the best ways to counterbalance those negative thoughts and feelings is to tap into your belief in the power of love and kindness. Love and kindness can't solve every problem, but reminding yourself of their existence and empowerment can help you gain a more optimistic viewpoint and hopeful perspective.

You probably know the power of love and kindness from experience. Perhaps the love from your family members has made you feel secure and important. Most likely, you have received a kind word or gesture from a teacher, friend, or even someone you don't know, and its impact made your day brighter. Being the recipient of love and kindness is just one way to understand their power. Sharing love and kindness yourself can be powerful, too, and can strengthen your belief that these characteristics make the world a better place.

Everyone has moments in which they feel less hopeful. During these times, it's beneficial to think of the many examples of when love and kindness made a difference in your life. This will empower you to continue believing in these principles and encourage you to share love and kindness whenever and wherever you are able.

[52]
YOU LEAVE A MARK WHEREVER YOU GO

The idea of "leaving a mark" might seem odd at first. This doesn't mean that you are literally leaving a mark at the places you go, but rather that you have a positive impact on others and the environment around you.

Some people are under the impression that leaving a mark means doing something bold, unusual, or unexpected so others will remember them. These actions, however, are not necessary for you to be noticeable and memorable to others. People are more likely to have positive feelings toward and memories of people who are genuine, helpful, and considerate. These are all traits you possess and carry with you everywhere you go.

Certain elements in our society might lead us to believe that we must receive a lot of attention or have influence over others to stand out or be accepted. Social media can add to this type of pressure and skew our perspective in terms of what is truly valuable about an individual. It's important to remind yourself that the impression you leave behind has nothing to do with the number of people following you or wanting to be like you. The "mark" you make wherever you go comes from who you are on the inside and how you treat others.

[53]
YOU KNOW HOW
TO PICK YOURSELF UP

A "setback" is a problem or difficulty that interrupts your progress toward a goal or destination. Everyone experiences setbacks at various levels. Therefore, it's what we do in the face of a setback that determines our outcome.

Some setbacks are minor and cause just a slight delay or inconvenience. For example, if you are practicing each day for an upcoming tennis match and it rains for 24 hours, the inclement weather would only be a minor, temporary interruption in your practice and on the journey to your ultimate goal. Unfortunately, some setbacks can create much more of an impact and present obstacles that are difficult to overcome. Examples of these types of setbacks might include illness, financial problems, or natural disasters. When it comes to minor setbacks, it's often best to just pick yourself up and get right back on the path to your goal. Major setbacks might take more time, effort, and out-of-the-box thinking before you can continue your journey.

Knowing how to pick yourself up after a setback, whether minor or major, means that you are determined to follow your dreams and pursue your goals. Keeping a positive attitude and believing in yourself will keep you strong along the way, even if you have to adjust your timetable, strategy, or objective.

[54]
YOUR AMBITIONS ARE FUELED BY YOUR SPIRIT

An "ambition" is something you strongly wish to achieve through hard work and determination. Ambitions are similar to goals and often require long-term planning and perseverance. For example, you might have an ambition to become a film director, a surgeon, or even mayor of your city. Though most people tend to associate ambitions with achieving importance in their career, social status, or notoriety, ambitions can certainly be smaller in scope and less complex. Some of the greatest ambitions are practical and attainable, such as earning good grades, increasing volunteer hours, or raising awareness for a meaningful cause.

Your ambitions are fueled by your spirit, which means they are personal. You have the drive and energy to fulfill your ambitions, whether large or small. This includes your spirit of perseverance, determination, and self-confidence, combined with your natural talents and the skills and wisdom you have developed through experience. Occasionally, we encounter people known as "naysayers" who tend to be pessimistic or skeptical about what others can accomplish. However, it's important to realize that your ambitions don't have to be influenced by anyone's thoughts or opinions. It is your internal spirit that gives them life—not any outside forces.

[55]
YOU'VE SHARED YOUR WISDOM GENEROUSLY

You already know you are a person who seeks knowledge and wisdom. This gives you what is called "insight," the ability to have a deeper appreciation and understanding of a person or situation. For example, your wisdom regarding effective time management might give you the insight that studying all night for a test the next day is counterproductive compared to studying for small intervals each day before the exam.

When you are generous in sharing your wisdom and insights, you can help others see situations more clearly and develop a better understanding. This is especially helpful if you have faced a certain challenge or been through a particular circumstance that someone else hasn't. Your experience and knowledge in these cases provide you with a perspective that can help others avoid mistakes. Older siblings, mentors, and parents often have excellent intuition, which makes their observations and insights valuable.

Occasionally, others might not want to hear your wisdom and insights. This doesn't mean they don't trust you, but rather that they might feel the need to figure things out on their own. In these cases, you can take comfort in knowing that you will be there if they decide to reach out for your thoughts and advice and that you are generously giving them space in the meantime.

[56]
YOU'RE PROACTIVE

Being proactive is a trait shared by many successful and fulfilled people. When you are proactive, it means that you take the initiative and put yourself in charge of your life. The opposite of proactive is reactive, which indicates more of a "wait and see" mindset. Proactive people are adept at looking forward, creating objectives, and analyzing circumstances so they are empowered to succeed.

Let's say you have an upcoming job interview for a position you really want. A reactive person might try to avoid thinking about it and just allow the interview process to run its course, accepting whatever outcome takes place. A proactive person might take the initiative of researching the skills required for the job, improving their resume, and practicing beneficial interview techniques such as good posture, eye contact, and confident body language. In this instance, being proactive means you have taken charge of the situation as much as possible and provided yourself with tools for success. Even if you don't get the job, your proactive nature will be a reassurance that you were prepared, and you'll be ready to try again.

Some situations are unforeseen and limit our ability to be proactive. In these cases, we might have no choice but to be reactive. However, it's important to know that when you take charge of your life as much as you can, you'll feel more empowered to handle these reactive situations and find a positive outcome.

[57]
YOU SEEK OUT
SOLUTIONS

Sometimes, we think about our problems so much that we "dwell" on them. This means that we become preoccupied with worry or stuck in a loop of negative thoughts about the issues and challenges we face. Though it's reasonable — and even beneficial — to think about our problems, dwelling on them can be unhealthy. That's why finding solutions to our problems is a much better approach than constant worry.

Certain problems have straightforward solutions. For example, if you find that you are spending too much time online with social media, you can solve that problem by limiting your screen time to a specific interval each day, with no exceptions. In this case, it's important to fill that time with other activities such as reading, taking a walk, or even volunteering. By replacing your problem with a solution, you benefit from choosing more productive behaviors that will keep you from reproaching yourself for and dwelling on lost time online.

Other problems, unfortunately, are not as easy or simple to solve. Understandably, we find ourselves dwelling on bigger and more complex problems, such as money or relationship issues, because their presence might be hard to ignore. However, becoming stuck in a loop of thinking about our problems rather than trying to find ways to take action will only prolong the situation. In these cases, your strength will be to find small solutions to lead you forward, making problems more manageable and keeping you on a path of progress.

[58]
YOU SPREAD
JOY

Another reason you are an awesome person is because you spread joy through your deeds and words. This means that you create happiness in others with what you say and the actions you take. Each time you do or say something generous or kind, you create an opportunity to spread joy to others and make the world better, no matter how big or small.

Spreading joy is often associated with holidays, especially Thanksgiving and Christmas. At those times of the year, people are reminded to feel gratitude, give to others, and share happiness. However, you don't have to wait for a certain season to spread joy. Each day comes with opportunities to make someone feel happy, even just for a moment.

For example, you might smile at someone on the bus who seems to be feeling rushed or stressed and lighten their mood. Or you might do something thoughtful at home for your parents to make the household more joyful. Even giving your best friend a genuine compliment out of the blue is a way to spread joy. You might never know the full positive impacts of your words and deeds but understanding that you create happiness around you will fill you with joy as well.

[59]
YOU BELIEVE IN YOURSELF

Believing in yourself and your abilities is the best way to develop and maintain self-confidence. Some people might confuse this confidence with arrogance, but they are quite different. Arrogance is a prideful, outward feeling that some people have in thinking that they know or are capable of more than other people without evidence to support it. Self-confidence is more of an internal feeling of knowing your skills and abilities well enough to accept and trust yourself in most situations.

Belief in yourself and self-confidence not only allow you to follow your dreams and achieve your goals, but they also help to keep your mind open to new possibilities and opportunities. For example, you might be aware that you have excellent problem-solving skills but be unaware of how much fun you would have in a robotics program. Self-confidence in your abilities can lead you to try things that can open new worlds.

Believing in yourself and your abilities also means that you can acknowledge your limitations in a healthy way. It can be difficult for people to learn to say "no" when they are asked to do something that they don't wish to do or that they don't have the time and resources for. Your confidence in yourself not only allows you to accomplish your dreams and goals but can also keep you focused on what you value and believe to be truly important. This will give you the ability to set clear boundaries and politely decline activities that don't match your interests.

[60]
YOU RESPECT
OUR PLANET

In many ways, humans are more aware than ever of their impact on the Earth and its living beings. Our relationship to the planet, its resources, and other life forms grows more complex as the human population and technology expand. Unfortunately, this can lead to negative outcomes for plants, animals, and overall health. Thankfully, many innovative and resourceful people are working to counteract some of the damage that has taken place and prevent further issues. In addition, with growing awareness, most individuals have good intentions toward the planet and the life it supports.

Sometimes, the political discussions and scientific data regarding climate change and its effects can feel overwhelming and the problems insurmountable. However, the fact that you cherish and respect our planet and its many forms of life is a great start to doing what you can to protect the environment. We can do many little gestures each day to reduce our impact, such as recycling, limiting our use of plastics, and conserving energy whenever possible. In addition, many organizations help volunteers make a positive difference in environmental matters, both locally and globally.

Thinking about climate change can indeed create anxiety, especially for those who care so deeply about life on Earth. If you feel this way, remember that most people are doing their part as individuals to be respectful of the planet and its creatures, and those efforts combine to make a positive impact now and in the future. When you express your feelings to those you trust, you're likely to find that your concerns and hopes are shared, which can provide you with comfort and optimism in addition to the motivation to take action. Be proud of the individual you are and all the ways you work each day to protect this precious world.

[61]
YOUR HUGS HAVE HEALING POWERS

It might surprise you to learn that giving and getting hugs is the most common source and demonstration of comfort among humans, but hugging has significant physical, emotional, and mental health benefits as well. Therefore, your hugs have actual healing powers.

Hugging someone, whether a friend, family member, or acquaintance, has been shown to reduce stress in both parties, especially in painful or unpleasant times. Researchers have found that giving and receiving this affectionate gesture can help alleviate pain and anxiety. Hugs can also enhance the health of your immune and cardiovascular systems.

Some people are more naturally prone to give and/or accept hugs. In many cultures, hugging is a big part of greeting or saying goodbye to someone. However, not everyone enjoys being hugged, so it's important to recognize a person's body language to determine if they are open to such physical expression. If you wish to hug someone, but you aren't sure whether they are receptive, it's reasonable to ask, "Can I give you a hug?" That way, you'll know for sure how they feel, and they will know that you care about their feelings.

Ultimately, your hugs have healing powers due to the feelings that they create in others. Hugging releases oxytocin, a hormone associated with happiness and stress reduction. In addition, the touch of a hug provides a physical connection and a certain type of expression that words and other gestures can't quite match. Hugs are a method of communication, and when you give one, you are providing reassurance, support, and comfort.

[62]
YOUR JOURNEY INSPIRES OTHERS

Though it sounds cliché to compare life to a journey, the metaphor makes a lot of sense. Most of us follow many paths and directions, with several obstacles, detours, and stops as we progress through the days, months, and years of our lives. Your journey, and in particular the goals you set and work to achieve, is an inspiration to others. For example, you might have friends or younger siblings who are inspired by your dedication to a sport, instrument, or other activity. As you follow each path with passion and determination, you might lead them to do the same with their interests. Even people who are "further along" in their journey, such as the adults in your life, are likely to feel appreciation and inspiration for the chances you take and the successes you earn.

You might have several people in your life who can offer guidance, motivation, and support as you make your journey. These can include parents, grandparents, teachers, mentors, friends, coaches, and siblings. Any combination of these individuals would likely add up to a strong network of people who care about and want the best for you. However, it's also important to remember that your short- and long-term hopes, dreams, and goals are personal. In other words, if your intuition and inner direction don't seem to match what others think, it's good to maintain belief in yourself and follow the path that reflects your true self. This will keep you inspired and help you be an inspiration to many others.

[63]
YOU CONSTANTLY CHALLENGE YOURSELF

It's often said that people are their own worst critics, meaning they have harsher standards by which they measure themselves than others. A healthier approach to this type of self-talk is to be more like an internal coach or teacher, challenging yourself in positive ways to do better by working hard, embracing opportunities, and motivating yourself to achieve your goals. This is a strategy used by many successful people who encourage themselves to reach their personal and professional best.

However, challenging yourself to do better doesn't mean that you question your abilities or undermine your confidence with negative self-talk; it simply means that you seek opportunities to improve and develop. For example, if you enjoy playing soccer and wish to join a higher-level team, you might challenge yourself to practice for a certain amount of time each day or complete exercises to build your strength and endurance. If you want to get better at playing the piano, you might select a more complex piece of music than what you are used to and decide to play it for your family when you are ready.

It's healthy to create a balance between challenging yourself and doing things purely for enjoyment. Not everything has to be a competition, even against yourself, and it's perfectly fine to accept that nobody can excel at everything. When you set personal and professional goals, you'll have clarity regarding the areas in which you will benefit from challenging yourself to do better and the areas in which you can relax and just enjoy.

[64]
YOU MAKE PEOPLE FEEL SEEN AND HEARD

Though we tend to interact with more people than ever, much of our interpersonal relationships and exchanges are through digital forms. This includes text, email, social media, and even visual communication platforms such as Zoom. Though these interactions are primarily positive, some people might find it difficult to genuinely feel seen and heard when they communicate in these ways.

The idea of feeling "seen and heard" can seem confusing if you take it literally because we are usually aware of when others can see and hear us. However, this particular phrase is more abstract; it means that someone has acknowledged your presence or communication in a significant way and that understanding is shared. When you make someone feel seen and heard, you are affirming their importance as a person. This helps build meaningful connections, brings clarity to communication, and encourages both parties to be themselves.

There are many ways that you can make people feel seen and heard. One of the clearest methods of doing so is to give them your full attention. This means avoiding distractions, such as your phone or other devices, and validating their communication with encouraging responses and relevant questions. Active listening is a big part of this process. Ultimately, when you give others your respect and attention, you are making them feel seen and heard. This not only improves your relationships and interpersonal skills, but it builds empathy, confidence, and leadership skills that will serve you well along the journey to happiness and success.

[65]
YOU VALUE EXPERIENCES OVER POSSESSIONS

If we step back and take a look at our culture through the lens of the media, it can be shocking to realize the extent to which we are influenced to buy material things. This can come in the form of anything from a television commercial promoting the luxury of purchasing a new car to a poster in a store that advertises brand-name clothes. The pressure to buy and own things is nothing new. However, as life gets more complicated and expensive, it's understandable that you would grow to value experiences over material possessions.

Experiences, as opposed to material things, involve spending time and energy doing something that creates memories, can be shared with others, and brings a sense of fulfillment. People who travel to see other places and cultures often value the experience far more than any souvenir they bring home. Experiences can also be individual or collective. For example, you might decide to take an art class to learn and explore your talents, or you might join your friends in running a 5K race and then celebrate together at the finish.

We often don't have anything tangible or material at the end of an experience (unless you count pictures or videos), but the memories of what we did tend to last far longer than any possessions we might collect. The value you place on experiences, whether individual or in a group, is what creates lasting joy, meaning, and personal satisfaction—which material possessions rarely offer.

[66]
YOUR LOVE TRANSFORMS LIVES

You have had, are having, and will have an impact on many people in your life. They might be inspired by your determination, encouraged by your smile, and even energized by your confidence. However, your love has the greatest power to transform the lives of others. When you show your love to someone, it is a gift of acceptance, trust, and appreciation. Not only does receiving love make others feel special, but it also replenishes their spirit and sense of self-worth. This can lead to positive transformations that will spread like ripples in water as your love and theirs continue to grow.

Your love and passion for what you value is another way you have likely transformed lives. When you invest your time and energy in making the world around you a better place out of love for your community, the environment, and your fellow humans, there is a strong chance that you are creating positive and impactful change. For example, you might organize a beach clean-up in your area out of the passion you feel for keeping plastics and other items out of the ocean. This might inspire others to become involved, making the area safer for humans, animals, and marine life. These positive changes can add up to larger transformations in the lives of others—all thanks to the love you have to share.

[67]
YOU'RE A BEACON
OF HOPE

A beacon is generally known to be a stream of light that serves as a signal to others. Most people associate beacons with lighthouses, designed to draw attention to land and safety for those sailing in the water. Though you aren't literally a beacon of light, your positive outlook can serve as a signal of hope and optimism for others in trying times.

It can sometimes be difficult to know that our loved ones or others are going through hardships. However, we often feel deep empathy for people who experience troubling times, especially if the circumstances are out of their control. In feeling this empathy, we might also feel inadequate to provide the necessary help or support to ease someone's difficulty. That's where your beacon of hope can come in and bring a sense of optimism or reassurance.

Just your presence in the world and the way you care for others can lighten someone's burden and lessen their worries.

Not only are you a beacon of hope for other people, but you can also be a source of hope for yourself when life becomes challenging. Your optimism, belief in yourself, and determination can help sustain you and enhance your resilience in times of sadness or struggle. Thankfully, across time, life tends to balance good and bad moments. That's why maintaining and setting an example of hope is so important. You will be far more successful in navigating and enduring the trying times — and helping others do the same — by allowing your optimistic outlook to shine.

[68]
YOU HAVE THE COURAGE TO BE VULNERABLE

Someone is vulnerable when they allow themselves to be open, either physically or emotionally. Most people are reluctant to be vulnerable in front of others because of the risk of being hurt, rejected, or shamed in some way. This can happen because of another's intentional or unintentional reaction. Some people encourage and support our vulnerability by letting us know they are accepting and trustworthy. For example, you might be comfortable being vulnerable in front of your parents, your best friend, or someone else you feel has consistently demonstrated respect and care for your feelings.

Examples of being vulnerable include admitting a mistake and apologizing, taking a risk, sharing something personal, and sharing your emotions. These actions require openness and courage because there is a chance others might not understand, empathize with, or support you in the way you hope or expect. Even the people in your life with the best of intentions might react in an uncomfortable or awkward way, especially if they are unfamiliar with showing vulnerability themselves.

People with the courage to be vulnerable are willing to trust others by being open. This means allowing someone to see you in a deeply authentic way. To protect yourself, you should have an established level of trust before becoming truly vulnerable to someone else. In addition to the courage it takes, being vulnerable also requires personal strength and resilience. These qualities are special because even if people don't react to your authenticity in the way you expect or wish, you have the inner confidence to remain true to yourself and be proud of your courage.

[69]
YOU VALUE
SELF-CARE

One of the most important principles for physical, mental, and emotional health is self-care. This means taking time and action to support your body's wellness, such as getting quality sleep, maintaining a nutritious diet, and exercising on a regular schedule. However, self-care is not just about focusing on what keeps your body in good health. Your mental and emotional well-being are equally important and require just as much care and attention.

There is an impression that self-care means occasionally treating yourself to something like a spa day or shopping trip. These are certainly nice activities, but they are more of a distraction. True self-care involves regularly being in touch with your thoughts, feelings, and physical state. For example, if you notice that you feel burned out by too many social commitments, it's important to take a break and prioritize your needs. You might also realize that being online for too many hours is causing you stress or sleep deprivation. In this case, getting away from screens by reading a book or spending time outdoors in the fresh air would be a good form of self-care. There is nothing selfish about taking care of your physical, mental, and emotional health. The better you take care of yourself, the more you will be able to share your life positively with others.

It's also important to keep in mind that part of self-care includes reaching outside yourself for supportive resources when you need them. If you are feeling overwhelmed for any reason, be sure to speak to a trusted adult. Sometimes, it can be hard to discuss our issues or ask for help, but many people in your life are willing to provide the support you need or find helpful resources—just as you would for others.

[70]
YOUR WISDOM
EXCEEDS YOUR YEARS

We've addressed the fact that you are a lifelong learner who seeks knowledge and wisdom. The wisdom you already have is likely beyond your years, meaning at a higher level than most would expect at your age. This is empowering because it allows you to apply your learning and experience to your current and future self. Your wisdom enhances your perspective and ability to solve problems and can guide you through challenging situations and difficult decisions.

Though you can't expect your wisdom to lead you to perfect choices—or any other type of perfection—you can be confident that it is a beneficial tool that will continue to develop over time. This means you will likely stay ahead of the curve and increase your chances of success and happiness in the long term.

Keep in mind that even though you have wisdom beyond your years, the best way to maintain that wisdom and develop it further is to continue pursuing knowledge and new experiences. This means recognizing and taking opportunities to expand your knowledge and participation in meaningful interests so your wisdom will grow along with you.

[71]
YOU APPRECIATE THE SIMPLE THINGS

People are so busy that they often forget to notice the simple things that make life so wonderful. Being preoccupied with everything we have to do, where we have to go, and all our other responsibilities can cause us to miss the wonders of the world around us. That's why it's so special that you notice and appreciate the simple pleasures in life.

One easy way to appreciate life's simple pleasures is to take moments each day to pay close attention to the five senses: sight, sound, smell, taste, and touch. These senses allow our brains to gather and process information about the world around us, but they also offer us the chance to recognize life's pleasures at a very basic level. For example, you might appreciate the fresh smell of clean laundry, the gentle sound of a windchime, the soft feel of your cat's fur, the sweet taste of an apple, or the sight of your friend's smile. Taking in these simple moments of appreciation can make a big difference in restoring calm to your thoughts.

There are many ways to appreciate the simple pleasures in life and many simple pleasures to appreciate when we take the time to notice. This not only reminds us to feel gratitude, but it can also provide balance for our emotional and mental health. We are overwhelmed with information about the world each day, and much of that can be quite negative. Solutions to big problems often seem insurmountable. However, when we stop to appreciate the beauty and simple pleasures around us, our outlook becomes more positive, and we feel more calm and hopeful.

[72]
YOU SUPPORT
YOUR LOVED ONES

One of the reasons your loved ones appreciate you is that they know you are a source of support. Your kindness, compassion, and open heart invite those you love to seek your guidance, comfort, and encouragement. Your supportive nature strengthens the relationships you have with family, friends, and other meaningful people in your life. It also conveys that you are a trustworthy, respectful, and considerate person.

You can offer support for your loved ones in many ways, big and small. For example, if you have a friend who is struggling with an academic subject that you happen to excel in, you can offer to help explain concepts or provide some tutoring. Another example would be offering a smile or hug to a sibling who feels a bit down. Active listening, encouraging words, and even just being present for someone you love are also ways of showing your support, care, and compassion.

Remember that although you are an amazing source of support for your loved ones, you also need to be a source of support for yourself. There's a common saying that "you can't pour from an empty cup." This means that, in order to be there for those you love, you need to be sure that your needs are met first. Self-care is a big part of prioritizing your health and well-being, so you have the energy and strength to encourage, help, and comfort your loved ones when they need it.

[73]
YOUR ACTS OF KINDNESS CHANGE THE WORLD

We are often so wrapped up in our daily tasks and schedules that we might not notice the impact and effect we have on others and our environment. However, we leave a lasting impact on the world through our actions, behavior, and attitude. A large part of understanding this is considering the way people might remember us or the contributions we have made to our relationships and communities.

When you treat others with respect and appreciation, whether you see them every day or only once, you are making an impact. Showing love and kindness to others adds to this and will leave others with the impression that you are a caring, generous, and thoughtful individual. Even if your actions or gestures are not formally acknowledged or celebrated, you can feel assured of your positive imprint on the world and the people around you. The more people you meet and the more time you spend sharing your love and kindness, the stronger your impact will grow.

[74]
YOU'RE CURIOUS ABOUT THE WORLD

Part of the joy of being a lifelong learner is embracing curiosity. Curious people tend to have more positive emotions and stronger relationships as they engage more closely with others. In addition, seeking a greater understanding of the people and world around you keeps your mind active and enhances your critical thinking, problem-solving skills, and creativity.

Being curious and seeking a better understanding of the world is another way of developing empathy. As you know, empathy is the ability to view things from another person's perspective, understand their emotions, and feel compassion toward them. When we wonder about others and their experiences, it encourages us to share their viewpoints and feelings. This not only gives us a deeper and broader grasp of another person's journey, but it also increases our self-awareness.

Some people confuse curiosity with being nosy or intrusive, but there is a big difference. Curious people are open, active learners with the goal of gaining a better understanding of concepts. Nosy or intrusive people are typically interested in information that someone else feels is private. Your curiosity comes from a desire to expand your knowledge and wisdom to grow as a person. Maintaining your curious nature and drive to understand the world will strengthen your intellect, relationships, and empathy for others.

[75]
YOU HAVE A BOUNDLESS CAPACITY FOR LOVE

You have a boundless capacity for love, which means that you allow yourself to feel love in all its forms and for everything possible. Sometimes, it's hard to imagine that our love is without limits. However, the more you understand the value of giving and receiving love, the more you will realize the endless capacity you have for it.

Humans can feel and express many types of love. There is romantic love, which is commonly portrayed in movies as a relationship based on a level of attraction and infatuation. However, love more often comes in the form of friendship, caring, and personal passion. For example, you might love your best friend as if he is your brother rather than limiting the capacity of love you have for him to someone outside your family. You might love your school, sports team, or community in such a way that you care for it as you might for your home or neighborhood. In addition, you might have a strong passion and love for reading that leads you to volunteer at the library and help others develop the same appreciation.

When we open ourselves to give and receive love in all its forms, we are likely to realize that our capacity for love is without boundaries. This means that the source of your love and the ways you express it are endless as well.

[76]
YOU UPLIFT OTHERS

An important part of what makes you an awesome person is your ability to uplift others with your words and actions. This means that you have the power to create positivity and optimism in others through what you say and do. For example, you might perform an act of kindness that lifts someone's spirits, such as holding open a door if their arms are full, or you might bring a smile to your sibling by wishing them luck on a test. When your words and actions are genuine and kind, you can make a big difference in the way others are feeling and their perception of certain experiences.

Your words and actions have the power to uplift others and spread happiness by providing inspiration, comfort, and encouragement. The effects might not always be noticeable or returned the same way in the moment, and there might be times when you don't feel that your words or actions are enough to lift someone's spirits or lighten their mood. However, even on days when you aren't consciously trying to spread positivity, it's important to remember that your presence in the world, along with your caring and generous spirit, is enough.

[77]
YOU UNDERSTAND THE POWER OF NOW

Human beings tend to procrastinate, which means delaying or postponing an action. It can often seem easier or preferable to put off doing something until a later time, especially if it's a difficult, uncomfortable, or even boring task. Though this behavior is natural, it doesn't usually work in our favor. Waiting until the last minute to complete a task can be a source of stress and anxiety that further interrupts productivity and becomes a vicious cycle. It can also come with high costs, such as lateness, poor performance, and missed opportunities.

That's why it's awesome that you understand the power of now, taking action in the moment, and not letting the tasks you need to do build up to a stressful or overwhelming level. Those who are empowered to act in the moment realize that even small steps toward progress are beneficial and rewarding. They allow themselves to prioritize, focus, and eliminate distractions so their time and energy are put to effective use. The power of now is one of the best concepts we can learn to build self-confidence and reduce anxiety.

It's in our nature to procrastinate sometimes, so you shouldn't be hard on yourself if this happens. For example, you might decide to put off a school assignment until the weekend so that you can relax on a weekday and catch up on your favorite show. These small instances of choosing the "later" rather than the "now" are fairly harmless and can actually be healthy. The good news is that you can get right back to harnessing the power of now once you've recharged and accomplished the things you need to do so that you have the time and energy to achieve your goals.

[78]
YOU BUILD A LEGACY OF KINDNESS

Earlier, we talked about love and kindness and how it impacts the way people remember you. Kindness, in itself, is a legacy you leave behind long after you are present in a community or friend group. When people think of a legacy, they often picture the fame, renown, possessions, or money that someone leaves behind. However, everyone leaves a legacy in some way through the memories they create with others and the lasting impact they have on their environment and community. For example, you might have had a teacher when you were younger who encouraged you to express yourself through writing or think about a subject in a different way to better understand it. The shared inspiration, caring, and positive impression made by this teacher on your thoughts and feelings is part of their legacy.

There is no doubt that you have already made an impact on the people in your life and the community in which you live, and you will surely continue to do so. One of the brightest aspects of your legacy is that it is built on acts of kindness. These acts can be big gestures such as volunteering your time at a pet shelter, raising awareness of supportive programs in your community, or fundraising for an important cause. However, it's often little acts of kindness that can have the greatest impact, such as offering someone your seat on the bus, genuinely thanking a service worker, or doing a chore at home without being asked.

Maya Angelou, an American poet, once observed that "people will forget what you said, people will forget what you did, but people will never forget how you made them feel." When you build your legacy on acts of kindness, people will remember that you made the time and effort to offer them consideration, goodwill, and compassion in large or small ways. This thoughtfulness will create a positive impression of your legacy in their minds and hearts.

[79]
YOU RADIATE CONFIDENCE

The confidence and self-assuredness that you radiate means that others can sense your optimism, self-trust, and self-reliance. Confidence and self-assuredness serve us in many beneficial ways. These characteristics can help us feel capable of facing challenges and taking advantage of opportunities. They can also help us be resilient in overcoming setbacks. As you radiate confidence and self-assuredness, you will inspire trust, support, and respect from yourself as well as others.

Some people might confuse your air of confidence and self-assuredness with arrogance or pride, but keep in mind that there is a big difference. Your confidence reflects a belief in yourself in addition to an awareness of your capabilities, skills, and experiences. Unlike arrogance, showing confidence and self-assuredness is not a way to attract attention or appear self-important. Self-assured people don't feel the need to exaggerate or brag about their accomplishments or abilities. Instead, they naturally and positively express a sense of self-worth and self-esteem that inspires appreciation and confidence in others.

There will be times when you don't necessarily feel confident or self-assured — and that is entirely reasonable and normal. It's important to allow those moments to run their course and show yourself compassion. For example, if you are starting a new job or activity, it might take a while for you to learn the skills that are required and feel sure of your abilities. As long as you are open to learning, patient with your progress, and believe in yourself, your confidence and self-assuredness will return in no time.

[80]
YOU RESPECT AND EMBRACE DIVERSITY

As you already know, every individual is unique. This means that, by definition, we are all different in some ways than every other person on the planet. Our differences are what often lead to progress, creativity, liberty, and empathy. However, it can be difficult for some people to understand and appreciate the range of human diversity, which is why those who embrace and support the individuality of others are essential in protecting human freedoms.

Diversity includes all the ways people can be different. In general, diversity often refers to age, race, gender identity, systems of faith, national origin, ethnicity, physical abilities, or political affiliations, though these are not all the ways people are different. When we embrace diversity, it means that we acknowledge, respect, and accept that others have different beliefs, attributes, perspectives, and approaches to life. This is more important than ever so individuals and groups can be allowed the freedom to be and express who they are.

When you show that you respect differences among all people, you are modeling strength and empathy. Unfortunately, some people fear or feel threatened by the unknown and unfamiliar. This can lead to prejudiced opinions or sweeping judgments about others that are not based on reason or direct experience. Embracing diversity doesn't mean that you have to like everyone in the same way or support harmful behaviors. It does mean, however, that you understand that to be different is to be human — and that is an awesome quality.

[81]
YOU'RE A DREAMER
AND A DOER

Some people might separate the world into dreamers and doers, meaning that some dream about what they'd like to do, and others do things rather than dream about them. Each of these characteristics is admirable, but the fact that you are both a dreamer and a doer is an ideal and awesome combination.

As a dreamer, you use your imagination and consider all possibilities. This might include dreaming about your future relationships, career, or hobbies. Dreamers tend to think big and view an overall picture as opposed to breaking ideas down into smaller tasks. They are typically creative, innovative, and visionary. Yet dreamers might be less efficient or organized in following through with necessary steps. As a doer, you set goals and take action to achieve them. Doers are often naturally productive, motivated, and progressive. They tend to avoid procrastination, yet they might spend so much time focusing on what needs to be done that they miss opportunities along the way.

It's important for you to nurture both your dreamer and doer sides for a healthy balance and approach to life. When you embrace your inner dreamer, you can allow yourself to imagine and think creatively to discover your passions and purpose. This can lead to ideas and opportunities that you haven't considered before. Then, your doer self can process how to achieve the goals that reflect what you have dreamed. This combination will ensure a fulfilling and exciting journey for your future.

[82]
YOUR COMPASSION
SHOWS THROUGH ACTIONS

One of the most important and rewarding characteristics a human can possess is compassion. Being compassionate means that you are aware of, sensitive to, and concerned about others' hardships or misfortunes. Compassion is rooted in empathy and caring. It allows us to understand and connect with people on a deeper level, which builds relationships and community. When your compassion is evident in your actions, this reflects your emotional awareness and your desire to reach out and create a greater state of well-being for those in need.

Most people feel compassion for others who are struggling, but they might not know how to convey their sympathy or directly show their willingness to help. Big actions can be taken as a means of showing compassion, such as volunteering your time or donating money to a charity. However, smaller, daily acts of caring can often make the biggest difference over time. For example, your compassion is evident when you are kind to others, actively listen to them, offer to help with a task, and forgive their mistakes. In many ways, accepting people for who they are without judgment is one of the most compassionate acts we can achieve.

Our compassion is often inspired by world events that seem almost impossible to fix, such as natural disasters, poverty, or war. This can create feelings of helplessness or discouragement in terms of what an individual can do to help. However, it's important to remember that your actions have positive impacts that show your empathy and make a difference in the lives of others. In turn, this can inspire more acts of compassion that will certainly make the world a better place for everyone.

[83]
YOU LIVE WITH
PURPOSE AND INTENTION

Living with purpose and intention means that you are a mindful person who actively takes charge of what you do each day. This can mean setting short- and long-term goals and taking active, meaningful steps to achieve them. Living with purpose and intention also reflects a conscious feeling of gratitude for the positive aspects of caring people in your life.

When you live with purpose, you demonstrate a proactive approach to your life. You understand that you have goals you would like to reach as well as the drive and ability to achieve them. Someone's life purpose is often related to their passions and values. For example, you might feel very strongly about proper care for animals. This purpose can lead you to volunteer at a shelter, organize a drive for helpful resources, or even choose veterinary medicine as a career. Most people live their lives with many purposes, such as being responsible citizens, good friends, and lifelong learners. When you live with purpose each day, you move ever closer to reaching your goals.

When you live with intention, you are actively aware of your responsibilities and impact. This means you make conscious decisions to pursue your path and create positivity while also expressing gratitude for those who support and care about you. For example, you might decide to ask your teacher, coach, or employer for a letter of recommendation. To show your appreciation, you might take the time to write a thank-you letter for their leadership, support, and thoughtfulness. Living with intention can also mean avoiding procrastination and other passive behaviors. When you live each day with intention, you become an active participant in life. This allows you to embrace rewarding opportunities and stay mindful of your important relationships with others.

[84]
YOUR GENEROSITY KNOWS NO BOUNDS

Generosity is considered a virtue by most people because it reflects the goodness in humanity. Though we often associate generosity with giving gifts, money, or other material things, it is a concept that encompasses far more meaningful gestures. When you have a generous spirit, it means you are willing to share your time, attention, expertise, support, and other resources with those who might be in need. Unlike material items, your generous spirit is unlimited and can provide boundless benefits to others.

Another way you can show generosity is to avoid demonstrating or harboring a withholding spirit. This means that you do your best not to deny or resist expressing things like love, appreciation, and forgiveness. Generous people are not petty, greedy, or ill-intended. Instead, they offer acceptance, support, and encouragement whenever possible without expecting something in return.

Though your generous spirit knows no bounds, it's important to be aware of those who might try to take advantage of this admirable quality. In other words, there are some people who, unfortunately, might exploit your willingness to give. For example, you might offer to cover a shift for a co-worker so they can attend a family gathering. Most likely, your co-worker would be appreciative and possibly offer to reciprocate in the future. However, some people might disregard your kindness and just expect you to cover for them whenever they demand it. In cases like this, it's healthy to set boundaries so you can remain true to yourself and not feel obligated to someone who does not respect your giving nature.

[85]
YOU HAVE A BEAUTIFUL SOUL

People often associate the word "soul" with a religious or spiritual connotation. In this case, the word "soul" means your inner nature and innate qualities—what makes you who you are. When people recognize that you have a beautiful soul, it shows that they are aware of your kindness, acceptance, and generosity toward others. The fact that your soul shines brightly reflects your willingness to share your inner beauty and strength with the people and world around you.

When people describe someone as having a beautiful soul, it means the person is naturally genuine and compassionate. They are also likely to be nonjudgmental and radiate peace and positivity as well. People with beautiful souls tend to be sensitive to what surrounds them, and appreciative of the little wonders life brings. For example, you might consider teachers, caregivers, and other openhearted individuals to have beautiful souls. These qualities are part of who you are on the inside as well, and they shine brightly for others who are near enough to experience your thoughtfulness and welcoming spirit.

People with beautiful souls are not always perfect. Even those with the most caring nature are allowed and expected to have negative moments or difficult days when they feel less giving or selfless. Having a beautiful soul means that you are forgiving and compassionate toward yourself and others during such times, with the knowledge that you will continue to be as kind and generous as possible and spread your positivity in the future.

[86]
YOU'RE CONSTANTLY GROWING

There are many ways you demonstrate your constant growth and willingness to push your limits. One example is the way in which you keep an open mind and spirit as a lifelong learner. The more we gather and integrate our knowledge and experiences, the more growth and understanding we attain. This leads to increased empathy and compassion that can bring a more fulfilling purpose to your life and inspire new passions as well.

In addition, as you make progress and strive toward more goals, you develop a stronger sense of confidence in who you are and what you can do. This keeps your mind and heart open to new opportunities that might enhance your growth even further. People are often fearful or reluctant to make changes, such as in their careers, relationships, or academic studies. There is comfort in knowing what to expect from familiar routines and experiences. However, this can create stagnant patterns that limit your passion and growth, leaving you in a rut.

It takes courage to push your limits and embrace new or different things. The belief you have in yourself, your inner strength, and your resilience will help you maintain that courage. For example, you might decide to push your physical limits and take up rock climbing. Believing that you are capable of learning the proper techniques and undergoing the appropriate training will give you the courage to try this new activity. Rock climbing might become a passion that leads you to meet new people and travel to different areas, or you might realize that it's not a good fit for you and a different activity would be more suitable. Ultimately, by allowing yourself to grow and push your limits in many ways, you will develop a deeper understanding of who you are and what you find rewarding.

[87]
YOU'RE FULL OF SURPRISES

One of your most awesome characteristics is that you are full of surprises. This keeps life interesting for you and the people around you. It also encourages a lifetime commitment to learning and trying new things. You might find that you have hidden talents or interests that you otherwise might never have unlocked.

One way that you are full of surprises is that you are open to a variety of opportunities and experiences. Many people prefer to stick to what they know or feel comfortable with to avoid the risk of disappointment or failure. However, you are willing and confident enough to take chances outside your comfort zone. This can lead to unexpected rewards, connections, and interests that make for a more fulfilling life. For example, you might decide to learn a new language, join a dance class, or visit a museum. Not only are you likely to surprise yourself, but you will probably surprise and encourage your friends and family to seek unique opportunities as well.

People often become set in their ways and routines. Though this can be effective for managing daily life, it can also interfere with keeping things interesting and fresh. You can commit to making your life interesting in many ways without compromising your responsibilities or traveling far away from home. One way to expand your learning, interests, and perspective is to visit the library and check out a new author or subject matter. Maintaining friendships and spending quality time with loved ones is another way to keep life interesting. A good strategy might be to set a goal to try something new and surprising each month and then follow through with it. This will keep you full of surprises and make your life exciting.

[88]
YOU'RE THOUGHTFUL AND CONSIDERATE

Just one of the many reasons you are awesome is that you're thoughtful and considerate. This means you are aware of others and treat them with as much kindness and respect as possible.

A big part of being considerate is having empathy and understanding the way other people around you are feeling. For example, you might know that your mother needs a few minutes to herself to recharge after work. One way to be considerate of her feelings and show your appreciation would be to do a small chore that eases her burden, such as helping prepare part of dinner or folding the laundry. On the other hand, you might notice that a friend is feeling frustrated about something and is not eager to engage in small talk. In this case, giving your friend some space indicates that you are mindful of their feelings. Little acts of consideration and respect for others can have a big and positive impact on those around you.

Many people use the words "thoughtful" and "considerate" interchangeably. They are indeed similar in that they involve an understanding of others and the desire to show kindness. However, thoughtfulness is typically developed over time, whereas consideration is often based on an awareness of and reaction to something that occurs in the moment, such as thanking someone for doing something nice for you. In general, thoughtfulness involves being considerate through intentional thinking beforehand. This might include remembering your best friend's birthday, showing interest in your brother's music, or even bringing a favorite snack to your coworker. Your thoughtfulness shows that you have intentionally taken the time and effort to get to know the people in your life at a meaningful level. This not only makes them feel special, but it deepens the connections within your relationship.

[89]
YOU'RE BRAVE

Sometimes, when we are challenged, it seems like it would be much easier to retreat, give up, or ignore the situation. Most people prefer to avoid confrontations or difficult circumstances. However, these conditions are inevitable, so knowing that you are brave and capable of facing challenges head-on is an advantage that will help you develop strength and continue to make progress.

You might have heard the expression "failing to plan is planning to fail." This is a simple way of saying that a good portion of success, or at least avoiding failure, depends on preparation, organization, and anticipating challenges. When you are brave enough to not only anticipate challenges but face them head-on, you are far more likely to achieve your goals and be successful. This doesn't mean that you will easily navigate all problems or difficulties that arise, but you will be prepared to use your critical-thinking skills and wisdom to overcome such obstacles.

Some people might think the idea of facing challenges head-on indicates an instinct to charge blindly into situations, ready to fight. However, that is far from the truth. People who directly confront challenges are not actually confrontational. Instead, they are self-confident, strategic, and thoughtful in their approach. You can think of facing challenges like you would navigate a new video game. Rather than just blasting your way through, your success likely depends on learning strategies, understanding positive and negative interactions, and developing patience as you progress. Real-life situations can differ greatly from video games, but the same smart and brave approach can help you successfully face and overcome challenges.

[90]
YOU VALUE
THE TRUTH

One of your awesome qualities is the way in which you value the truth and live with integrity. Having integrity means that you are honest and naturally follow strong moral principles, even when nobody is there to see. Living with integrity is closely related to respecting yourself and others. Your self-respect encourages you to be genuine and do what you feel is right as a means of staying true to yourself and your values. This also applies to your respect for others and the desire to treat them with genuine regard, fairness, and consideration.

People who value the truth are not only honest and sincere, but they tend to have open minds and compassionate hearts. As we get older and wiser, we realize exactly how complex people and events are. Sometimes, there isn't a singular truth to a situation; it is dependent on what your perspective is. The way you value the truth allows you to remain open and empathetic to different perspectives without judgment. In addition, this quality encourages you to gain knowledge and wisdom so you can develop a deeper understanding of the world and its people.

Valuing the truth and living with integrity are part of what makes up your character. Your character reflects your personality and behavior, specifically, your reliability and moral strength. Everyone has flaws and makes mistakes, but if truth and integrity are part of your character, you will have compassion and understand that the world is made up of complexities and diverse viewpoints.

[91]
YOU'RE A
REFLECTION OF LOVE

There are many different forms of love, and you will experience giving and receiving all types of love during your life. Just being who you are means that you are a reflection of love in its purest form. This includes your generous spirit, open heart, caring nature, and all the other wonderful qualities you possess.

There are some days when you might feel as if you are overflowing with love from others and some days when you might feel less so. This is to be expected, just as many things in life ebb and flow. However, on the days when you don't feel quite as loved or lovable, it's important to remember that many people in the world care about you just as you are, simply because you exist. Your family members, friends, and others who know you might not directly express their love for you with words each day, but you can be certain that they feel it. Their actions are often stronger in reflecting their love than words can be. People demonstrate love in many ways, from giving a hug to sending a funny text.

Another reassurance that you reflect love in its purest form is your capacity for self-love. Loving yourself doesn't mean that you feel arrogant or better than others. Instead, self-love is a healthy way of acknowledging the unique person that you are and appreciating all you contribute to the world. Understanding self-love in its purest form will encourage you to treat yourself with compassion, kindness, and care—just as you would the loved ones in your life.

[92]
YOU RECOGNIZE THE INTERCONNECTEDNESS OF LIFE

As we get older, we realize just how closely connected everything and everyone is in this world. When we recognize the interconnectedness of all things, it allows us to appreciate life's beauty and fragility.

We understand from birth how important connections are with people. We depend on others for almost everything in childhood, and as we grow, others come to depend on us. Our relationships provide us with love, support, and care and teach us to reciprocate. You are connected to an exponential number of people through your relationships with family, friends, teammates, co-workers, classmates, neighbors, social media members, and so on. Therefore, it is important to treat others with respect, kindness, and compassion, as this can have a ripple effect throughout the many communities of which you are part.

We are also connected to our environment and the planet itself. Our actions have an impact on the Earth and all forms of life. For example, if someone litters outside, their unsecured trash might cause harm to an animal or bird. At the very least, their litter would reflect a disregard for nature. When we consider how our actions might affect other lives, it encourages us to be mindful of our environment and avoid creating harmful situations to the best of our ability.

Understanding the interconnectedness of people, nature, and the environment not only inspires us to appreciate the world around us but it can also move us toward being better global citizens. In this way, we can strive to live in a respectful, compassionate, and caring way to have a positive impact.

[93]
YOUR PRESENCE BRINGS COMFORT

Certain people in the world naturally bring comfort and peace to those around them, and this is a special quality of yours as well. Just by being yourself and being present, you provide others with a sense of calm, support, and harmony.

People who have a peaceful and comforting presence are often described as "nurturing." This means they have a natural tendency to encourage, protect, and care for others. You might consider several people in your life to be nurturers, including your parents, grandparents, coaches, and teachers. They have likely played a role as caregivers or supporters to you in some way. Just as these individuals provide a sense of comfort and peace for you with their presence, you do the same for others. Nurturing is closely related to empathy and the ability to recognize how others are feeling and when they need comfort or support.

When we see that someone we care about is struggling, our instinct is typically to try and help them by finding solutions or alleviating their troubles. These are certainly great inclinations that are likely to be appreciated. However, there are various circumstances in which we can't offer someone direct help or a resolution to their problems. In these cases, it's important to remember that your presence alone can bring comfort and peace. The kindness and compassion you show through your support, active listening, and just being there might be exactly what is needed to ease someone's mind and heart.

[94]
YOU HAVE AN UNBREAKABLE SPIRIT

To have an unbreakable spirit means that you are determined, perseverant, and resilient. This is especially important when facing hardships, challenges, and disappointments, as we all do. For example, you might find yourself struggling to land a part-time job with flexible hours so you can also play a sport after school. This might cause you extra stress or make you feel discouraged. However, with an unbreakable spirit, you can remain optimistic and patient that there is a good fit for you out there in terms of employment if you keep looking or that you will have the creativity to consider alternatives that will provide the same results.

In addition to innovative thinking and persistence, other aspects of an unbreakable spirit include standing up for what you believe in, keeping your goals and passions alive, and being your own person. When you are inspired by your values, individuality, and the future, it allows you to deal effectively with potential setbacks or obstacles. This part of your unbreakable spirit can also fuel your self-confidence and self-assurance in knowing that you are committed to what you believe is right and determined to follow your dreams.

Having an unbreakable spirit doesn't mean that you won't experience disappointment or feel discouraged at times. When this happens, however, you can call upon your resilience and perseverance to either regroup and continue or find another path toward success. Focusing on the pursuit of your goals, being true to your beliefs, and allowing yourself to shine as an individual are all ways to boost your spirit so that it remains unbreakable when confronting difficulties.

[95]
YOU'RE A BEACON
OF POSITIVITY

Your positivity and optimism shine like a beacon for others. This is just one reason why people appreciate your beautiful soul and generous spirit. Most people feel increased happiness and comfort when they are near someone who has a positive outlook. This doesn't mean that you don't accept that there are flaws and difficulties in the world. Instead, it means that you believe in effective problem-solving and the opportunities that can come with challenges. By keeping an optimistic perspective, you inspire others to think positively as well.

It's perfectly fine to go through times when you feel less optimistic. Everyone struggles with difficult moments or periods when it might be hard to feel cheerful or confident about achieving success.

The important thing to remember is to maintain hope. Research has found that feeling hopeful has enormous benefits when it comes to our health and quality of life. These include reduced stress, increased happiness, stronger relationships, and even a greater likelihood of positive outcomes. Hope can influence the way we view our inner strength and the goodness in the world, which leads to more self-confidence and belief in others.

So, not only can your positivity and optimism be a beacon for others, but it can also be a beacon for you and a reminder to remain hopeful. In this way, even difficult circumstances or darker moments won't seem insurmountable, and you can draw on your resilience and self-assurance that your journey will end up successful.

[96]
YOU BELIEVE PEOPLE ARE INHERENTLY GOOD

Sometimes, it can be difficult to believe that most of the people in the world are good, especially when we are bombarded each day with information and stories of crime, corruption, prejudice, and more. However, it's important to remember that most people wish for peace, safety, and acceptance on an individual level, and many live their lives trying to achieve this for themselves and others. This is where you can find an unwavering faith in the goodness of people.

To balance the perception that much of the world is made up of people with poor intentions, it's important to be mindful of the generosity and caring shown every day by those around you. When you increase your awareness of kindness and compassion shared among others, you'll find examples of this behavior everywhere. You might notice strangers smiling at each other, someone offering to help another person, or even an individual going out of their way to cheer someone up who appears sad. It's also important to keep in mind all the people who love and support you with goodness in their hearts, from family members and friends to teachers and neighbors.

Having an unwavering faith in the goodness of people doesn't mean you should blindly trust others no matter what. In other words, your faith in the goodness of people reflects your belief that most individuals have heartfelt, positive intentions and don't wish to cause harm. Yet, trusting that everyone is likely to choose and act with integrity and goodness is, unfortunately, unrealistic. Therefore, it's important to be optimistic about people overall but also remember that they must earn your trust on an individual level.

[97]
YOU SEE CHALLENGES AS OPPORTUNITIES

Everyone faces challenges, some bigger than others. Often, our success in overcoming challenging times, situations, or events is partly dependent on the way we perceive them. If we view a challenge as an opportunity for growth, learning, or improvement, we are much more likely to achieve a positive outcome and feel better about the experience.

A challenge is typically known as a situation in which a person faces an obstacle they must overcome to reach success. Sometimes, these obstacles are literal, such as an injury, illness, or other interference. Other times, obstacles are more abstract or figurative, like anxiety or fear. When you are in the middle of a challenge, it might be hard to see it as an opportunity for something positive — especially if you are doubtful that the outcome will be successful. This is where your confidence and belief in yourself can play a large role in the way you face and frame your circumstances.

If you consider the many challenges you have overcome in the past, you will likely realize that you have an inner strength and adaptability that allows you to navigate obstacles on the path to success. In addition, these challenges can lead to opportunities for you to grow and learn, which you can apply to your present and future situations. For example, chemistry might be a challenging subject for you. You could look at this circumstance passively and just assume that you aren't good at that type of science, or you could recognize it as an opportunity to take charge of your learning and join a study group or ask for help from the teacher. If you can view challenges as opportunities to improve and learn, you will build your inner strength and find the path to success.

[98]
YOU CARE FOR
THE WORLD

One of your best qualities is the unlimited love and care you extend to the meaningful people in your life. You nurture many significant relationships each day, sometimes without even realizing it. This includes your family members and friends who benefit from your ongoing encouragement, affection, and support. Just being a loving and caring presence in the lives of those close to you can make a big impact.

Your love and care also extend beyond your inner family and friendship circle. This includes the love and care you extend to animals, the planet, the well-being of your community, and more. As we grow to appreciate and value our environment, we develop the capacity to love and care for the many wonders that make life special and magical. This not only expands our gratitude but also leads us to be better global citizens in how we treat and respect all life forms. Your loving and caring nature allows you to follow through on your dreams and extend your passion and purpose beyond boundaries to make the world a better place.

It's also important to apply love and care to yourself, just as you would to others. This might seem like a strange concept at first, but practicing self-love and self-care is the best way to achieve and maintain physical, mental, and emotional health. Without supporting your well-being, it can be very difficult to extend love and care to others, so make sure to nurture your body, mind, and heart each day through healthy behaviors. This will give you the strength, peace, and stability to extend your love and care beyond any boundaries.

[99]

YOU'RE A TREASURE TROVE OF EXPERIENCES

"Treasure trove" is a phrase that typically describes a collection of things that are wonderful and valuable. Your memories and experiences are collected inside your mind, heart, and spirit, which makes you a treasure trove of unique knowledge and insight. All these memories and experiences belong to you and have done their part in shaping who you are.

Your memories are like snapshots and short stories of the people and events in your life. Thinking about these memories is a way of identifying what has made an impact on you and how you've processed it. Memories are beneficial because they provide us with connections that can last long after an event is over, or someone has passed. They are also a wonderful way to feel and generate gratitude. For example, you might remember a teacher you had as a child who inspired you to love reading. Experiences can become memories, though our brains don't store much of what happens to us on a daily basis. However, the significant and meaningful things you go through, like a special vacation or the first time you met your best friend, are likely to be captured as memories.

Unfortunately, not all your memories or experiences will be positive, and some might be downright unpleasant. These memories and experiences play their part in shaping you as a
126

person as well, yet this doesn't mean that you should dwell on them. In other words, you are a complex blend of recollections, impressions, and feelings that have made up your life story so far, and each day, you add to this amazing treasure trove.

[100]
YOU'VE MADE THE WORLD A BETTER PLACE

It's easy to get the impression these days, especially from social media, that everyone is striving for notoriety or attention. Even the term "influencer" has come to represent a desirable career of sorts in which people are paid to promote products or establish trends. Unfortunately, focusing on the power or ability to influence can create a distorted perspective of what it means to have an impact on the world or make it a better place.

It might be difficult to imagine, but your presence in the world, by itself, makes it a better place, and whether you have any "followers" doesn't even matter. Your family, friends, co-workers, teammates, classmates, and community all benefit from your existence. This is because you are kind, loving, fun, and generous. You have a peaceful spirit and a compassionate nature. All the qualities that make you who you are also bring positivity and joy to everyone around you.

As we've established, you will automatically leave a positive legacy wherever you might be. As long as you are true to yourself and your values, respectful and considerate of others, and live with intention as much as possible, you don't need to be concerned with your impact or influence. Just your presence in the world makes it a better place, and it will continue to do so.

[101]
YOU ARE YOU,
THE MOST AWESOME
REASON OF ALL

Hopefully, by now, you understand just some of the many reasons you are an awesome individual. One book couldn't possibly list or contain them all. Your inner strength and beauty complement your outward kindness and empathy. You are made up of memories, experiences, relationships, and natural abilities that form a unique person, and you will continue to grow and learn to become wiser and more special each day.

Keep in mind that it's one thing to read a list of characteristics that make you awesome, but it's another to internalize these traits. In other words, all the collected and blended attributes that make you who you are should become part of your self-belief and mindset. This doesn't mean that you won't make mistakes or experience disappointments and setbacks; it means that you have earned self-assurance and a positive mindset for the future. No matter where your journey takes you and the challenges you might face along the way, never doubt your inner strengths, abilities, and beauty.

CONCLUSION

Remember, you are a mosaic of experiences, emotions, talents, and dreams that make you wonderfully unique. Embrace your strengths, acknowledge your growth, and celebrate the journey that has brought you to this moment.

Your worth extends far beyond what can be contained in these pages. You are capable of achieving extraordinary things, and your presence in the world adds immeasurable value. Each day presents an opportunity to shine, learn, and grow into the best version of yourself.

Continue to cherish the reasons that make you special. Embrace your quirks, nurture your passions, and remain open to experiences that enrich your life. You have the power to make a difference, inspire others, and create a world filled with kindness, empathy, and positivity.

As you close this book, carry with you the belief in your abilities, the confidence to face challenges, and the courage to stay true to yourself. You are an integral part of this ever-evolving tapestry of life, and your uniqueness adds vibrancy to the world around you.

Always remember: You are loved, valued, and undeniably awesome. Your journey of self-discovery continues, and the possibilities for greatness are infinite.

So, go forth with determination, kindness in your heart, and a belief in your awesomeness. The world eagerly awaits the incredible contributions only you can offer. Thank you for taking this journey with me. Keep being your awesome self!

www.ingramcontent.com/pod-product-compliance
Lightning Source LLC
Chambersburg PA
CBHW060237030426
42335CB00014B/1503